Anthony J. Drexel (Anthony Joseph Drexel Biddle

Word for Word and Letter for Letter

A Biographical Romance

Anthony J. Drexel (Anthony Joseph Drexel Biddle

Word for Word and Letter for Letter
A Biographical Romance

ISBN/EAN: 9783744665094

Printed in Europe, USA, Canada, Australia, Japan

Cover: Foto ©Thomas Meinert / pixelio.de

More available books at **www.hansebooks.com**

WORD FOR WORD

AND

LETTER FOR LETTER

HOW MY FATHER MET HIS DEATH.

WORD FOR WORD

AND

LETTER FOR LETTER

A Biographical Romance

BY

A. J. DREXEL BIDDLE

FELLOW OF THE AMERICAN GEOGRAPHICAL SOCIETY
AUTHOR OF "THE MADEIRA ISLANDS," "A DUAL ROLE AND OTHER
STORIES," ETC., ETC.

ILLUSTRATED BY EDWARD HOLLOWAY

LONDON

GAY & BIRD

22 Bedford Street, Strand, W. C.

1898

Philadelphia: Drexel Biddle, Walnut St.

Printed by
DREXEL BIDDLE,
Walnut Street, Philadelphia, U. S. A.

TO

MRS. ALEXANDER VAN RENSSELAER,

WITH MY AFFECTION

AND

HIGHEST ESTEEM.

CONTENTS.

PART I.

Down by an island beach I loved to wander
  In childhood's thoughtless years,
And o'er the sea to gaze.   Ne'er did I ponder
  On the world's hopes and fears.

In youth inquiring I grew ; the more I learn'd
  I yearned to know the more,
So, out upon the ocean's expanse, I turn'd
  My boat afar from shore.

PART II.

Tranquil was the water, the weather, balmy.
  I sailed the summer sea
In careless mood, until the skies grew stormy:
  And then, ah, woe was me!

A tempest wild arose. It broke, and, raging,
  Tossed my boat to and fro.
But back to the isle of my childhood, changing,
  I swept, willing or no.

PART III.

Here, in this island small, was all the treasure
  I'd gone abroad to find:
Indeed, a wondrous paradise of pleasure
  I once had left behind.

LIST OF ILLUSTRATIONS.

———

PART I.

Down by an island beach I loved to wander
  In childhood's thoughtless years,
And o'er the sea to gaze. Ne'er did I ponder
  On the world's hopes and fears.

In youth inquiring I grew; the more I learn'd
  I yearned to know the more.
So, out upon the ocean's expanse, I turn'd
  My boat afar from shore.

AB INITIO.

Young man, of the age of five and twenty, I had fallen heir to an estate of some five hundred thousand dollars through the death of my last remaining relative, Uncle Joshua Lefferts, my mother's brother.

Both my parents had died when I was very young, but there had always been a mystery connected with the death of my father. He had gone on business to Funchal, in the Island of Madeira, where, shortly after his arrival, he had been found one morning in his room at a hotel called "The Miles Carmo" (I always remember that name) with his throat cut. He had been assassinated: evidence, at the time, clearly proved this. But his murderer escaped. My father bore an honorable name, and his social position in Philadelphia was of the highest.

2

Shortly following my father's tragic death it came out that he had been robbed of a letter of credit which he had never had occasion to use. The letter was for the amount of twelve hundred pounds sterling, which entire sum, it was discovered, had been drawn at three of the various leading banks of Lisbon, Portugal, five days following the death of my father at Funchal. News travelled slowly in those days, for no submarine cable then connected Madeira with any of the continents.* So when the news of my father's death at last reached my mother by the slow process of the mail—which was, in those days, often sent circuitously from Madeira to the United States†—my poor father had been dead for some time; the Philadelphia bank, on being notified, found,

---

* The first cable to place Madeira within telegraphic connection with the world at large was laid by the Brazilian Submarine Telegraph Company in the year 1874. This line stretches, by way of Madeira, from Brazil to Portugal.

† In the early days of Madeira mail-service, letters for the United States frequently went first to Portugal, there to receive the government cancel before recrossing the broad Atlantic for the new world.

after considerable telegraphing, that this
letter of credit had been cashed some weeks
previously in Lisbon, as I have already
stated. Then a full description was supplied
the officials by the cashiers of the Lisbon
banking firms. No pains were spared on
the parts of the American and European authorities to catch the thief and murderer.
Indeed the matter became of international
importance for the while, and both the
American Consul and the Minister to Portugal became involved.

How well I remember the account which
my dear old uncle Joshua used so often to
repeat to me. It is engraven on my memory. I can see my uncle now, pacing to
and fro before the fireplace in his library.
With eyes fixed in a gaze as if to pierce the
gloom of mystery protecting my father's
murderer, he would say, partly to himself
and partly to me :—

"A Portuguese, without doubt, but a man
familiar with America and the American
banking system. A cunning fellow, I'll be
bound, and a man of good appearance and

address, they said. He spoke almost perfect English and used that language to address the different cashiers. Two of them took him to be an American, born and bred, and the third, who afterward testified to his accent as being Portuguese, had not the strength of purpose to state his opinion when he paid the money to the forger. Tall, slender, well-proportioned and of winning manners. Dark hair, swarthy complexion, black eyes!"

At this juncture my Uncle Joshua would always turn to me, and, with clenched fists, wildly denounce the murderer, expressing a wish to meet him face to face. "And your mother," he would say, "my own dear sister; the being whom I adored above my life: she was the sacrifice, for she died of a broken heart, only six months after the awful murder of your father." And then he would go on to tell me how my mother went to Madeira, taking me, at that time scarcely more than an infant, with her, and how he (my uncle) accompanied her in her sad quest there for her husband's body. They found it had been interred, through the kind interest of some of the British residents, in the cemetery adjoining the little English church.

On the voyage out my mother was taken seriously ill, and when Madeira was finally reached my uncle had a helpless invalid on his hands. Mother had taken the journey with the full intent of bringing home my father's body for interment in our family vault in the Laurel Hill Cemetery at Philadelphia. But this was not to be. Owing to her poor state of health, Uncle Joshua was obliged to take apartments for her at one of the hotels, and to postpone indefinitely the time of departure for home.

On her better days, when she felt any remaining strength or vigor, Uncle Joshua used to tell me that, contrary to the doctor's orders, she always insisted upon visiting my poor father's grave. But she pined away and died; and she was buried in the little English churchyard, by the side of her husband. Ah! well! I can recall but little of my parents, for I was but three years old when left an orphan, and in the guardianship of Uncle Joshua. . . . And now he was dead also.

Strange as it may appear, I had never gone to Madeira to visit the graves of my parents, but I was going now. Yes, I had fully decided, and I should start as soon as the cold weather set in.

In the description of myself which I have given, I have omitted several items that I should perhaps include:—

My name is George Lefferts Hall; I am not overburdened with remarkably good looks, though, if my dear friend Tyndall (whom I shall introduce later) is to be believed, I am "not a bad-looking chap." In height I measure five feet eleven inches, and I "tip the scales" at 170 pounds. I may style myself of the athletic school, for I am very fond of exercise, and, while in college, played upon the football and baseball teams.

CHAPTER I.

SUSPICIOUS CHARACTERS.

In chronicling my story, I would begin with the time of one of my visits to the borough of Holmesburg.

Having been to call upon Miss Emily Tracy, I was returning towards the railroad station about eleven o'clock in the evening. It was very dark, and when I stepped from the country road on to the main thoroughfare I sought the light of a street lamp to consult my watch.

Whence I had just come there emerged two muffled figures. They paused, looking cautiously about, and then passed over the street and continued down the cross-road I was about to take myself.

Verily suspicion seeks the mind at dark-time as readily as the bat flies into a lighted room through open windows.—I imagined that these receding figures slunk away with

the air of having been guilty of some mis-
deed. "And," thought I, "they have come
from the direction of the Tracy's." I found
myself picking my way quietly after the
two receding figures.

It was still a good five minutes' walk
to the depot. A vacant lot stood by the
roadside: I was prompted to turn off and
run swiftly through it. I came out at
the farther end upon the road again, and
ahead of the two men. They were not long
in coming up, and, having hidden myself
behind some bushes, I waited for them to
pass. As they came abreast of my hiding
place I peered cautiously out. I started as
I looked. Dark though it was, I could see
that one of the men had a very horrible
face: it seemed out of all natural propor-
tion. Just then the two halted; one struck
a match and lit a pipe, and, by the momentary light thus afforded, I plainly distinguished the other's countenance. But
was it a countenance? I shall never forget
my sensation at that moment. The man
had an oblong head on which rested a red

worsted cap; his face was of a purple hue, while his features were so distorted and fat that they fairly rolled about and shook like gelatin. He spoke, and his mouth twisted uncontrollably, his long, thick lips curling and flapping as he moved them.

"Yew git to tawn as quick as you can," he said. "The train leaves in five minutes, and there be no time ter stop fer pipe lightin'!"

"To the d——l with you," the other man replied. "How dare you hurry a gentleman! You'll get your money all right. And don't compel me to soil my hands on your ugly face, you unclean beast."

By this time the match had been tossed away, and I could only see the outlines of the men.

"Beast, unclean beast!" fairly shrieked the unfortunate misshapen creature, thus cruelly addressed. "Dis is de end to it all. I would hev been yer father-in-law—d——n me, ain't I yer father-in-law? Ef I ain't, it's because ye'r the low lived coward an' thief thet ye are. Yew go spyin' on women.

Yew ruined me daughter. Yew want to wreck another puir girl's life, and yew want me ter help yew, an' now yew call *me* an unclean beast!"

Here the voice of the other individual interrupted :

"Shut up, and don't be such a d——n fool, Griffiths. You know I can put you behind the bars to-morrow if I want to, for your part in the Tracy business."

Tracy business! Then my suspicions were correct. When I first saw these men they had stepped out from the road that led to the Tracy residence. Then they had been up to mischief in this direction ? I was again all attention, in my hiding place.

"You recollect the time you murdered that city gent who had come out here to 'do the grand' and who you found had done your wife the kindness to make his lady-love? Well, I didn't blab on you, and I was the only witness. But you know that I have it in my power to bring you to trial, at any time, for murder. I won't; it would hurt my own chances, but I won't support any child of your daughter's either. What's more, I'll go and see the woman now."

"Oh don't, don't!" cried the deformed being, piteously; "it will kill her ter see yew."

"So much the better," was the brutal answer. And with this the last speaker turned and strode down the road, while the misshapen man stumbled after him, still imploring him to stop and to change his purpose.

Without a moment's hesitation I stepped out from my place of concealment, and followed.

CHAPTER II.

ON again reaching the village the men turned off into a narrow little alley, where, as I had not followed closely for fear of being detected, I lost them for a short while. The alley, packed on either side with little wooden one and two story houses, evidently marked the poor quarter of the village.

Before an old rickety, tumble-down shanty stood a horse and gig. From its general appearance, I immediately concluded it to be a doctor's vehicle. Nor was I mistaken, for, as I directed my way towards it, a man appeared in the doorway of the shanty, and I heard a woman's voice from within call, in an uncertain, tremulous tone, " Don't stay away long, doctor."

Replying pleasantly, the individual turned and, jumping into his vehicle, drove off.

Scarce had the gig swung around the corner than I heard footsteps approaching. Instinctively, I hid myself in the shadow of the alleyway; and I was just in time.

From behind an angle of the building a man stole cautiously, and I saw that, as he stepped up to the entrance-way, opened the door, and went in, he was none other than the misshapen fellow I had followed. I crossed the way and took my stand at a place where a broken window-pane, patched with newspapers, might admit of some sound escaping.

I was not to be disappointed: soon I distinguished a low, agonized moaning within, which seemed to come at regular intervals; above this I could hear the excited voice of a man: I recognized it as being that of the unfortunate who had just gone in.

"I tell yew thet cursed Dooner's on his way here now," he said.

A sharp cry followed this announcement, and the voice of a woman called feebly out in protest. At this juncture my attention was once more turned to the outside, for I

heard some one running towards me. A
moment later a figure came up, passed
directly by, without observing me, and burst
rudely into the shanty. It was the other
man of the turnpike episode. His sudden
appearance was the cause of much commo-
tion.

The woman's voice called piteously,

"Ah, do not pursue me; leave me, leave
me!"

In brutal and profane words the newcomer addressed the suffering woman; he
taunted her, and then it seemed that he
struck her; there was a low wail of intense
fear and pain. There seemed to be no inter-
vention, so, unable to restrain myself, I
sprang at the door, threw it open, and rushed
into the house.

I found myself in the atmosphere of an ill-
ventilated room, dimly lit by two flickering
candles. Upon a couch of straw lay a young
girl, whom I could see was very beautiful.
Over her leaned the scoundrel. He looked
around quickly at me, an unexpected newcomer, and a vicious expression crossed his

face. I saw he had a broken nose and bristly red hair, and that he was squarely and powerfully built. Suddenly he began to tremble, and he became ashen-pale. "Mr. Hall!" he exclaimed; and I, in astonishment also, at his knowing my name (for I could not recall having ever seen him before), felt for the moment uncertain how to act.

A woman, attired in nurse's garb, stood at hand: from her ruffled appearance, I judged she had been attempting to come between the man and his intended victim.

Over in the farther corner cowered the man with the awful face.

Now the thought of calling on the police myself never entered my head. Probably the misshapen man did not do this for the reason that he whom he would thus deliver into the hands of the law, with the charge of assault upon his daughter, might then, in turn, testify against him in the matter of the murder. At least I gathered as much, considering that which I had overheard on the turnpike.

Again I looked at Dooner. He was en-

deavoring to reach the door unobserved;
and, as I saw this, my anger all came back.
I thought of the cowardliness of his brutal
assault upon the girl; though I had not
actually witnessed this assault, my imagination now painted it before me in flaming
colors.

Indeed, I was about to spring upon the
detestable fellow, when the suffering girl,
from her bed of straw, called to me and
thanked me for my intended protection,
while, at the same time, she implored me
"not to strike or attack Jack Dooner." I
felt a great shame come over me at the
thought of being in any way the cause of a
further disturbance in the chamber. So I
followed Dooner outside. He ran away, but
ere he had turned the corner I was after him.
Along the deserted village street I pursued.
He turned suddenly off into the very road
from which I had first seen him make his
appearance, with the misshapen man. Up
this road he plunged, and he had not run
far ere he reached the entrance-way to the
Tracy's. To my astonishment, he pitched

directly ahead, and I redoubled my efforts
to catch him, for he was making his way
towards the house. I called to him to stop;
having proved himself a sprinter of no mean
ability, however, he had now distanced me
considerably. Suddenly, I lost sight of him.
The darkness had grown intense, but I felt
that it would soon be dawn, for a fresh breeze
sprang up, such as, in summer, is usually
the forerunner of daybreak. Indeed, even
as I stood huddling myself in the chilly air
and deliberating, the blackness turned into
the gray of twilight. Now, I was familiar
with every nook and corner of the Tracy
homestead, for, being one of Miss Tracy's
admirers, I had been a frequent visitor. So
I searched the grounds for well-nigh an hour,
but not a trace could I find of the villainous
Dooner. The sun was by this time well up,
but the house was still closed and silent, no
one as yet being astir. Seeing and considering these things I departed for the railroad
station. Arrived there, I sank upon a bench
to rest myself; I was foot-sore and fa-
tigued. The only person about was a sleepy-

looking, half-dressed, station master. Of him I inquired concerning trains, and, finding that a train for town was due shortly, I asked him to flag it, which he did.

The car I entered was nearly vacant, so I stretched myself out, full length, between two of the seats, and dozed until the engine brought up in Broad Street Station.

CHAPTER III.

OF MY FRIEND TYNDALL.

At present I occupy apartments in a boarding-house on Walnut Street. Having breakfasted, I set out to look up my friend Tyndall. He was a young physician; and, though I do say it, whatever practice he had acquired since coming to Philadelphia, a perfect stranger, some two years previously, had been owing in large measure to the influence and aid I had given him. I had introduced him to all my friends, and had proposed him for membership to the several clubs to which he belonged.

To-day when I met Tyndall, he asked me abruptly why I didn't take a trip somewhere. In fact, for my sake, he said he was anxious for me to get away. He thought I needed a change. I did not inform him of my most recent visit to the Tracys', nor of

the adventures which befell me before my
return to town. It greatly astonished me,
therefore, when he told me he had learned of
my visit. I asked him who had been his
informant.

"Oh, a friend of mine that saw you there,"
he replied lightly, and winking at me know-
ingly.

I did not like his familiarity in this direction, for, though Tyndall said he had never
met Miss Tracy, he apparently harbored
some unaccountable prejudice against her.
This feeling on his part I had always re-
sented. But Tyndall had a keen percep-
tion, and I seldom had to inform him when
he displeased me.—Now, it so happened that
I had once presented Tyndall to a Miss
Blumer, a girl for whom I at times entertained an infatuation; and much to my per-
plexity, Tyndall had since seemed ever de-
sirous to turn my attention from Miss Tracy
to Miss Blumer.—On the present occasion,
however, he went so far as to suggest my
going to Newport, the summer-home of the
Blumers.

Of course I grew angry at such an attempt at dictation on the part of my friend; but, curiously enough, no quarrel arose, as Tyndall became very meek and apologized for having offended me.

And then, when I thought the matter over, Newport was a very alluring suggestion. I remembered that Miss Blumer had expressed the wish to see me. After all, why should I not take the jaunt? I concluded to go to Newport.

I neglected to question Tyndall again as to who his friend might be that saw me at the Tracys'. Afterwards I regretted this neglect.

James Brown Tyndall was some twelve years my senior. He was of medium stature. He had keen, piercing, steel-gray eyes, which were ever on the alert, and his face was broad, while his features, though not large, were clearly defined. He wore a short pointed beard which was of light brown color, and a heavy growth of dark brown hair covered his well developed head. Quite an adept in the art of hypnotism, he claimed that the knowledge of this power was of great advantage to him in the profession to which he was devoted. He said that he had often cured a critical case by bringing the patient to believe that he or she was not ill at all, but in good health.

CHAPTER IV.

SPIED UPON.

It was a beautiful August afternoon; as I stepped into the street, after my call upon Tyndall, I thought, "It is just the day for the country."

So I set off for the depot, and took a train for Holmesburg, bent upon a twofold mission: one of a pleasant, and the other of a disagreeable, nature. For, on the one hand, I was going to call upon Miss Tracy, and, on the other, I had resolved to pay another visit to the home of the misshapen man, feeling, as I did, troubled over my knowledge of the whereabouts of an undiscovered murderer.

The Tracys resided near Holmesburg, a village lying within the city limits; but the family were in few ways associated with city life. They lived on an old ancestral place, and rather to themselves, though they were fond of travel, frequently visiting Europe

and other foreign continents. Mr. Tracy
was thought to be very wealthy. He was
a man of letters ; and, though greatly sought
after, he mixed seldom with his fellow men,
caring little for society and less for clubs;
in consequence of which traits he was called
queer and unsociable. He had two charming daughters, the Misses Gertrude and
Emily; and his wife was one of the most
lovely women I have ever had the good fortune to know. She was dignified, sweet,
motherly, and withal possessed of that sympathetic freshness of spirit which, in an older
woman, is so charming a trait. The family
were sincerely hospitable towards those of
whom they were fond. But they were independent of society, and hence their circle
of friends was small, though select.

Alighting from the train at Holmesburg
Junction, I found myself in a quandary as
to whether I should first visit the murderer
or, on the other hand, should call upon the
Tracys. I had resolved to set out on my
disagreeable mission when I became aware
of the near approach of a horse and wagon.

I was standing in the road, before the station, at the time : a silvery voice called,

"Why, Mr. Lefferts, how-do-you-do!"

A moment later I was reaching over the wheels to shake hands with Miss Gertrude Tracy. She had driven down to the station to meet her father, whom she had expected to arrive by the train on which I had come. Being now invited to take the vacant seat beside her, in the dog-cart, there was nothing left for me to do, I thought, but to comply.

Is there ever a time for the feeling of greater pride, in the varied life of a young man, than when he is driving at the side of a beautiful young woman? If such an occasion is not for him one of supreme *happiness* then there can be but one of two explanations : either something is radically wrong with him, or he must be in love and cannot have proposed.

My fair companion was an excellent whip; she sat erect and, looking exceedingly handsome in her neatly fitting tailor-gown, conversed so entertainingly that I paid little heed to the course we were taking through the village.

At length she said,

" Emily is visiting Anne, a poor young girl who used to be a maid of ours. Anne lies very ill, and is in dreadful straits. Emily is such a queer girl; she does things that I wouldn't think of doing. No sooner had she heard of Anne's trouble than she must be down in the village, and working herself like a slave. She heard of the thing only last evening, just after you left our house, from a young woman, who said she was a next-door neighbor to Anne, and who added that she was acting as Anne's nurse, and that Anne had earnestly implored her to seek and bring dear kind Miss Emily to her before she died. This was the message; and so, early this morning, before any of us were up, the woman called again for Em, and she departed with her. She knew her: Em knows all the poor. *I* thought not 'dear, kind Miss Emily,' but foolish, imprudent Em, for Anne's father looks like a nightmare, and is the fright of Holmesburg."

"You should see him!" Miss Gertrude continued, as I tried to suppress my rising excitement. "But here we are," she said, pulling in the horse; indeed there we were before the identical hovel of my last night's adventure.

I sprang out, knocked upon the door, which was immediately opened, and out walked Miss Emily Tracy, looking radiantly beautiful, and as fresh and free from care as though she had never been in the presence of sorrow.

When she recognized me she gave a little start and blushed quite crimson with embarrassment: on perceiving who had brought me thither, she appeared exceedingly provoked. But at recovery of self-possession, when suddenly placed in an embarrassing position, a woman is more speedy than a man: and so Miss Tracy's embarrassment, forsaking her, took possession of me. In fact, she seemed to be talking both to her sister and to me simultaneously, as she sprang lightly into the cart and seated herself beside Miss Gertrude before I, in my

awkwardness, was sufficiently on the alert
to offer my assistance.

"Well, are you going to walk?" asked
Emily, with an amused twinkle in her laughing eyes, as I stood inactively, looking up at
her. I took the hint, and, joining as naturally as I could in the merry laughter of the
girls, I jumped into the back seat of the
cart; whereupon we drove off.

The sisters were delightfully contrasted,
being so totally different in their dispositions
and tastes, and yet, withal, so devoted.
There was no discordancy between them, of
the slightest character, and the respective
charms of each offset those of the other without clash or detraction. Never have I met
with such a sweet-tempered and gentle-
natured girl as Emily. In manner she was
free and open, and was complete in that quiet
dignity of bearing which is surely the sym-
bol of a pure and beautiful character. I
have, in slight measure, previously endeavored to describe Miss Gertrude. Though
agreeable, her tendency was, figuratively
speaking, to cut and slash in her conversa-

tion; one felt that he must be on guard while talking with her, for she was uncommonly clever at repartee and unmercifully candid in her opinions. She was a more conspicuous and striking looking girl than her sister, but, though not *over*-forward in her manner, she was not possessed of the unconsciousness of beauty, the retiring modesty, and the unselfishness of disposition which so characterized Emily.

On reaching the gates of the Tracy estate, our steed turned sharply in—as a horse invariably does when at the entrance to the place of his stabling—and we rattled up the cinder-covered and tree-lined avenue, towards the house. Halfway thither we met Mrs. Tracy, who had evidently walked out with the expectation of meeting her husband. Her face showed disappointment on her perceiving me in the place of Mr. Tracy. But when I sprang out of the cart, hat in hand, to make my apologies for calling so soon again, she said,

"Our friends are always welcome, and I am happy to see you, Mr. Hall."

It was shortly after this that I was walking, at the side of Miss Emily, down the garden path towards the lake. The lake lay at the foot of a gently sloping series of terraces, on the summit of which stood the Tracy mansion. At the end of the garden we passed through a rustic summer-house and down a long flight of wooden steps. Then we quickly reached the water's edge.

The setting sun reflected his sleepy evening glow upon us as I, having helped Miss Emily to a seat in the canoe, took my place with the paddle, and pushed the craft out upon the water. I need scarcely mention that I had been anxious to bring our conversation to bear on the subject of the misshapen man and his daughter. Now that the time for doing this seemed to have arrived, however, I was at a loss to know how to aptly introduce the topic. So, after several awkward endeavors at beginnings, which in each case I turned into a channel of meaning, other than that I had in mind, I gave up the attempt, and perhaps acted wisely in so doing.

Our conversation touched upon various

topics: Miss Emily casually remarked that her father had planned a trip abroad for the early part of the coming winter. At the time of receiving this interesting piece of information I paid little attention, for I had been too much absorbed in my own endeavors to introduce the subject engrossing my thoughts. Now, however, I saw that I had been almost rude when Miss Emily told me of her prospective departure abroad: and, as I was *really* interested,—in fact, more interested than I cared to acknowledge—I hastened to remark concerning it.

When I had done so Miss Emily replied,

"Why, Mr. Hall, you seem to be surprised. You know we go abroad almost every winter."

"I was not surprised, Miss Emily, but anxious; for I too am going abroad, and I do so hope it may be by the same steamer."

"Oh how fine that would be! it would indeed make a jolly party. When are you going? Gertrude would be so glad if she knew it."

"I was not thinking of your sister, Miss Emily; I was thinking of you."

At this Miss Tracy became slightly uneasy, and there was an awkward pause.

Then I started,—my eyes became riveted on a clump of bushes, at the opposite shore of the lake,—I had seen the bushes parted, and the face of a man peer cautiously out. That man was watching us; no sooner did I realize this than I looked quickly away again. For I felt instinctively that I should like to see more of him, and that I should not be successful in the desire did he know that he was observed.

Miss Tracy said,

"What in the world is the matter? You look too queer for words."

This took me aback; but I explained that I had seen a snake, and a snake always did upset me. She laughed heartily, and remarked that it was the first time she had ever known me to be afraid of anything. Now my pride was hit, but I smiled and said nothing further. However, I paddled in an apparently unconcerned manner in the direction of those bushes. Being in the stern myself, Miss Emily was seated, facing me, in the bow; and thus, by keeping the canoe headed for the object of my curiosity, I might investigate by dint of careful management, without Miss Tracy's observing: though I should have to be careful to allow no telltale expression on my face.

Within but a few rods of shore, I descried the man, crouched in the thickest part of the bushes. I was rather handicapped in my endeavors to get a good look at him, in that I wished he should not see I observed him, and that Miss Tracy should not become aware of his presence. Notwithstanding, a series of rapid glances discovered to me a startlingly perplexing fact: the man in hiding was none other than Jack Dooner, of last night's adventure. Perceiving this, I hastily backed water; for an impulse prompted me to get Miss Tracy as far away as possible from the proximity of this scoundrel. On reaching the opposite side of the lake I had, to some extent, recovered from my surprise. Then many questions crowded themselves into my bewildered mind. "Had Miss Tracy ever seen this Dooner? Did she know of him? Why had Dooner taken refuge in the Tracy place last night, and why was he here again? Could it possibly have been with the aid of some accomplice in the Tracy household that he disappeared from me here so abruptly last night?"

I wondered as to what Dooner could have meant last night, when I overheard him say to the misshapen man that he could cause his arrest "for his part in the Tracy business."

But a short time since I had found Emily at the house of the misshapen man: indeed, the recollection of her evident displeasure at this discovery of mine was a thought that fairly burned in my brain.

And now the impulse that came to me was to seek Mr. Tracy, inform him of this Dooner, and then ascertain what he might know.

But my next impulse, which I can only attempt to explain as being at that time natural to my very morbid disposition, was to say nothing of the matter.—I cannot gainsay that I became suspicious of the Tracys, though what object they might possibly

have to gain by setting a man to spy upon
me I could not even then imagine. Doubtless, like many a young man who unexpect-
edly falls heir and manager to a large estate,
my head was for the time turned by my good
fortune. And so I think that, at that period
of which I write, I had an irrationally large
opinion of my own importance, which made
me unreasonably careful of my interests.
Verily, I was a fool.—I have never forgiven
myself for the manner in which I acted on
this occasion. And indeed I have since
had bitter cause to repent. I decided to
escort Miss Emily back to her house, and
there to bid her a very good evening.

The family were seated on the front piazza
when we came up. Mr. Tracy had returned
home during our absence at the lake; and
he now stepped forward, with outstretched
hand and greeting of—what I thought—
unusual cordiality.

"Mr. Hall," he said, "you and my daughter have been to the lake?"

"Yes," I replied.

His face brightened. "Ah, it is the place

of all others I would have my friends visit :
it is my favorite haunt. There I can feel
safe from all intrusion ; and I have written
my best books by the banks of that placid
lake. I can assure you, sir, when you are
there you may feel certain of being unmo-
lested. But are you not going to stay and
sup with us ? " he inquired, as I continued
standing, and glancing uneasily down the
road, as though I would be off.

I made my excuses with as good a grace
as I could, and in the midst of my so doing
Miss Emily interrupted me :—

" Why, Mr. Hall, you told my sister that
you would remain for tea, and we have fully
expected you to do so."

" Thank you exceedingly," I replied, " for
your kind hospitality. But I have just recalled the fact that I have an urgent business engagement in town this evening ; and
I must be going."

Miss Emily looked at me steadfastly for a
moment, and then, with a sigh, she turned
away and entered the house. She gave me
no opportunity of bidding her good-bye.

MR. TRACY STEPPED FORWARD WITH A GREETING OF—WHAT I THOUGHT—UNUSUAL CORDIALITY.

Having made my adieus to the others, I departed. Arriving at the gates, I happened to look back, and my attention was attracted by a light shining from a third-story window; standing against the light I saw the figure of Miss Emily Tracy; though I could but distinguish her silhouette, I felt that she was looking after me.

A moment later I found myself out upon the highway, and moving in the direction of the village and of the home of the misshapen man.

CHAPTER V.

LIGHT UPON THE PAST.

I HAD waited for some minutes outside the closed door of the miserable little dwelling, now unpleasantly familiar to me. At length, as I was growing impatient, the door opened a small space, and a hideous face, which I immediately recognized, confronted me. A glance of mutual recognition being exchanged, my acquaintance of the night previous opened wide his door, and stepped out. I said I had called to see him on a matter of great importance; on hearing which he grew nervous.

"Won't yew come inside, sir?" he asked in words, though not in tone.

I saw I was not wanted, but I did not hesitate. Within, things were changed. In the place where the straw couch had been there was now a comfortable little cot; upon it lay the girl I had seen recently in suffering. She was now apparently sleeping. Thrown over her was a steamer-rug, on the corner of which I happened to observe two large red initials, E. T. Embarrassed at being in this room, I asked my host if there was none other. He replied in the affirmative, and led the way into a small kitchen adjoining.

Leaving the door between ajar, so that he might hear any sounds from the room where slept his daughter, he motioned me to a seat on the only chair visible, and settled himself near me upon an upturned wooden box. Leaning forward, in attentive attitude, he waited for me to speak.

I was not long in doing so. I told him, in a few blunt words, I had good reason to believe that he was a murderer; on hearing which he started to his feet, with a smothered oath, and then sank upon the floor, all of a heap, and trembling in every limb. Such action on being accused was conclusive of his guilt, I decided; and I paused that he might have time to recover some composure before I again addressed him.

But I was to be disappointed in that I had expected to be another time the first to speak. My unfortunate host regained his self-control as quickly as he had lost it. He arose, drew himself to his full height, and, looking me straight in the eye, addressed me, in a deep, hard voice:—

"Young gent, yew hev found me out, and I won't make no attempt at denyin's thet I killed a man. Whether I done a great sin in killin' of a man wot robbed me of all wot I had in this world an' all wot I hoped to hev, ef I wuz good enough, in the next, yew can best opinion fer yerself, when I hev told yew how I come ter do the awful crime.

"It wuz about twenty yearn ago, in the young days of the Burg,* thet a high tony gent cum out here ter live, and do the grand. He wuz a dandy in his dress an' manner.—But yew see, sir, I had a wife wot wuz a wife; she wuz called the most beauti-

---

* The abbreviation of the lower-class residents for Holmesburg.

ful woman hereabouts, an' she wuz very
gran' lookin', and thet's a fact.

"Well, the gent I'm tellin' yew about
wasn't long in learnin' of the awful devil
wot had the angel wife; thet's the way the
folks used to call us. Now, yew see I wuz
the butt of the village, an' of the country
round. Mothers scared their kids into bein'
good by sayin', 'Tom Ugly-Face 'll catch
yew.'—'Tom Ugly-Face' is me nom de
plum.—But I never used ter pay no attention to any of 'em. I always had a blessin'
fer them all, when she wuz livin', fer thet's
wot she taught me.

"She wouldn't never let me be revengeful,
an' we used ter read the Bible to each other
by the hour. Me wife brought the sun-
shine into me life, so thet I never cared wot
others said of me, an' I guess I wuz hap-
pier than most any man hereabouts.

"An' then when our daughter wuz born,
—thet gal in there, sir,—an' when me wife
an' me seen how beautiful she wuz, we
growed better than ever, fer we knowed thet
Heaven had blessed us by sendin' us a lovely

child. Them days when we had our little
baby wuz the happiest of me life. An' me
wife used frequent ter tell me, in comfort
ter me, thet the father's beauty, he had lost
in birth, wuz now found in his child. Yew
see, sir, I wuz born with me awful face, an'
I've always hed it. Why me wife ever
loved me is no more'n I kin tell than why
she married me. But she did love me, fer
she must hev loved me lots ter hev married
me. An' I loved her with me whole eternal
soul. Well, we lived on our lives with our
little one till this gent I'm tellin' yew of
come along. When he heard me wife wuz
beautiful, an' when he heard wot a fright I
wuz, I guess he thought he'd hev easy game.
He come roun' ter see us, an' wuz fer sym-
pathizin' with her on me bad looks. But
me wife wuz proud and loyal, an' she
wouldn't hev no sympathy ; fer she said as
how I wuz better lookin' in me soul than
him. She said it wuz the soul of the man
she looked to, not his face. An' so me wife
an' me lived, but we wuz simple folks. We
did feel high tony ter hev a gent an' a

dandy comin' visitin' us, which he did, an' always seemin' kind an' friendly. He spoke good English, but I knowed he wuz a furrener from furren parts, fer he had black hair, an' looked jest like a dago."

Here the misshapen man paused. This description rather startled me. I began to feel as though I were having a hideous nightmare, and as though the misshapen man, the spectre of my evil dream, were relating something oddly and disagreeably familiar to my memory. Was this forethought, or was I the subject of some hallucination? I could not decide, and I peered more intently through the gloom, and into the dreadful face of the strange narrator. Perceiving my increasing interest, he continued :—

"Well, sir, 't wa'n't long after Torres, fer thet wuz his name, had been gettin' so intimate with us, before I begun to notice a change in me wife. She seemed to hev grown hard on me, an' she would become listless-like whenever I wuz round. This made me feel awful bad, but I done me best ter keep up cheerful.

"An' now a change come. At first I didn't notice it, poor fool thet I wuz. Me wife stopped goin' ter church with me; she stopped takin' care of our little child, an' didn't seem ter love it no longer. An' still I tried ter keep up cheerful, an' I never said a disagreeable word, though me poor wife scolded an' ordered me roun' like a dog. Then I seen thet Torres didn't cum ter see us no more. But then I seen more too: me wife wuz away from home most of the time, an' she never asked me ter go with her when she went away. I wouldn't foller her, or spy on her, fer I loved her too much; an' I never let meself suspect her of anything neither. Then, one day, I found her holdin' me little gal up by the heels, an' tryin' ter swing her pretty head, thet hung down, against a tree. I run up an' grabbed me child, an' asked me wife why she acted like she did. She slunk away from me as though she hated me presence; an' she said nawthin' ter comfort me. Then the neighbors an' folks asked me ef me wife would soon be Mrs. Torres. I struck one man fer sayin'

this. But the folks kept up a plaguing me
so thet I become frightened for me wife. I
loved her distracted, sir, an' now she didn't
care fer me. I seen how she owned me soul;
fer she had told me years before thet thet wuz
wot she married me fer.—An' she still owns
me soul, an' always will, tew eternity.—
Well, one night she didn't come home, an' I
growed suspicious. I didn't sleep no more
at nights, an' I was always worryin' silently
an' by meself. 'Fer luck,' thought I, 'I'll
go to Torres' house an' look about, but I'm
sartain me wife *ain't* there.' So out I went,
an' up the road, ter where the dandy, Torres,
lived.

"He had a gran' house, an' when I come
up to it, I seen it all ablaze with lights inside. The shutters wuz closed, but the
light come through them. I went an' rung
the door bell, an' when the door wuz opened
by a young boy I heered the sound of music.
Then I heered a ringing laugh. Will I ever
forget it? It *wuz* me wife! I shoved the
boy aside an' went into the house. Goin'
through some gran' furnished empty rooms

I come upon me wife. She was dancin' ter
the tune of a music-box. Sittin' on a lot
of cushions an' lookin' up at her wuz Torres.
He was grinnin' at her, an' of a sudden me
wife stopped dancin' an' jumped right into
his arms. Well then they seen me, an' I
don't know which of the two of 'em wuz
most scared.

"Right in front of me wife, I asked Torres ef she had been to see him often. At
this Torres got mad, an' he jumped up an'
hit me an' knocked me down. An' yet I
did not touch him; but, when I had staggered to me feet, I stood up ter him, an' repeated me question.

"'Of course she's been here,' replied Torres. 'She's only a poor ignorant woman,
an' I'm about tired of her now, meself, so
yew can have her back again.'

"When I heered them words I was seized
with a blind fury. Me wife growed white
an' terrible to look at, an' Torres began to
tremble, fer he seed he wuz fooled in the
people he wuz dealin' with. Well, what I
done then I can't exactly remember, but I

know thet I giv' a big leap on top of Torres,
an' he had a knife ready fer me, dago thet
he wuz. But he didn't seem ter hurt me
somehow, fer I was fightin' like a devil, I
guess. I threw him on the floor, an' throt-
tled him, an' the next thing I knowed, I wuz
bein' hauled off him by the young boy wot
had opened the door fer me.

"I got up as ef I wuz dreamin', but
Torres didn't move. His eyes wuz starin'
out ov his head like bullets bein' shot from
a gun. I looked fer me wife, an' seen her up
in the far corner of the room. She wuz
starin' at me with the wild look of a crazy
person. I went over to her, but she shoved
me off. 'You've killed him!' wuz all she
said, an' she kept on lookin' at me crazy like.
Then I wuz scared ; but Torres wasn't dead.
He began ter squirm an' ter kick an' ter
mumble in a dago lingo I didn't understand.

"But he occasionally said a word or two
in English, an', as he jabbered a good while
before he got quiet fer good, I managed ter
learn thet he had killed somebody at a place
wot sounded like 'Madeery.' "

"Stop!" I cried; and I sprang to my feet, and paced the floor, in great excitement.

My loud ejaculation not only brought my host's story to a pause, but also roused an infant, in the sick-room.

I had been unaware of the presence of a baby when I passed through the room occupied by the misshapen man's daughter. But now an unmistakable baby voice rang out. The misshapen man repaired to the next room, for a few moments, and left me alone to my thoughts.

Now I knew that that which had struck me as forethought, when my host had first spoken to me of Torres, had been in reality a recognition of the description of my father's assassin, as I had so often heard that description from my Uncle Joshua. In a fever of impatience I awaited the return of my informant.

Before he could take up the thread of his story, I was plying him with questions concerning a fuller description of Torres.

" Was he tall ? "

" Yes."

"Slender?"

"Yes."

"Well proportioned and well made?"

"He was."

"He had black eyes and a swarthy complexion?"

"He had both, sir, an' yew seem ter hev knowed him yerself!" the man replied, in great astonishment. "But," he continued, "how in heaven's name did yew ever see the villain? An' ef yew did see him, how do yew remember him? Fer yew must hev been mighty young when yew *last* seen him, seein' he died more'n twenty yearn ago, at my hands."

"Be that as it may," I replied, endeavoring to calm myself somewhat—I did not wish that this self-confessed murderer should know the real facts concerning my knowledge of Torres.—"I once heard of a great thief whose description tallies precisely with the account you have given me of this Torres." I spoke thus, hoping to pass the matter over: but this attempt of mine to make light of my knowledge of my father's

5

assassin only had the contrary effect upon my host. He began eagerly plying me with questions. I saw that my best resort was to affect eagerness to hear *his* story out. I did so :—

" But you left off in the most exciting part of your history," I said, " I demand that, as I am a witness to the confession of your guilt, you tell me what followed after you had committed your crime."

Thus adjured, an expression of bitter hate came into the murderer's face. He drew close up to me, and I had to nerve myself, for his expression was horrible.

" Yew want me ter tell yew the rest," he growled passionately, " when I hev told yew all so fer, wot I needn't hev said beans about."

" I knew of your guilt before you told me," I replied, reminding him that I had said as much to him in the outset, and before he had confessed himself to me. At this he grew deeply remorseful in that he had corroborated the evidence of my belief in his confession.

AN EXPRESSION OF BITTER HATE CAME INTO THE MURDERER'S FACE.

"How did yew know?" he cried. "I only had one witness beside me wife, an' thet wuz Dooner."

"Was Dooner the young boy you spoke of?" I interrupted.

"Cert., an' ter think yew didn't know even thet. Oh h——l! wot a d——n fool I've been ter blab on meself. I calculate as how yer goin' ter tell the cops* an' testify agin me fer murder. I kin prove thet I killed Torres in self-defense, ef I want ter. An' here yer comin' houndin' me out ter throw me in jail, an' ter try and hev me swing,† ain't yew?"

As he said this he gave a hideous laugh, and then his expression changed, and he wrung his hands, in mingled rage and fear.

Afterwards I could get nothing further from him. When I asked him what became of his wife following the commission of his crime, he sprang toward me, and I stepped back a pace, thinking I should have to

* Cops, slang for police.
† Swing, slang term, meaning to hang, or to be executed.

defend myself against an onslaught. But
he stopped midway :—

" Yew kin hev me put behind the bars*
ef yew wants, may be, but yew *can't* make
me talk no more ter yew," he said. "An'
don't yew say no more about or agin' me
wife. She ain't dead an' she ain't here, but
yew can't talk about her.

" Before yew go, which I hope yew will
now, without disturbance, seein' the unsar-
tin condition of me daughter, I hev ter
thank yew fer yer prevention of me com-
mittin' another murder. Fer I wuz so near
a doin' it last night when yew come in an'
chased Dooner away fer a hittin' of me
poor gal, thet I hev been scared ever since,
an' I'm scared now ter think wot i'll ever do
when next I meets him. I'll tell yew one
thing, me fine gent, in concludin'. Look out
fer *yerself.* Yer bein' tracked an' spied on
when yew come out here ; though I'm
through with the business meself, since wot
yew did fer me last night, there be others

* Taken into custody.

wot ain't of my way of thinkin'. An' yew'd
better take good care of yerself, an' not go
to persecutin' me, wot gives yew a tip fer
yer future welfare. Still I feels yer goin' to
hunt me down, an' still I says *take care;*
fer I like yew, in spite of meself. Look out
fer a friend of your'n wot lives in the city.
He's tryin' ter do yew dirt* an' ter git yer
money. An' look out fer Dooner, an' look
out fer——" A feeble call from the next
room interrupted the speaker.

It was growing late. I decided to take
my departure then and there, and to return
to the murderer on the morrow, when he
might be in less stubborn frame of mind,
and when, moreover, I might have gained
time to consider what I should do concerning my knowledge of his crime; for this
weighed heavily upon me. Accordingly, I
made my way from the hovel, and to the
railroad station. Here I arrived just in time
to catch a train bound for the city.

* "*To do a person dirt*" is a vulgar way of saying, *to
betray one's confidence, or to blackmail.*

CHAPTER VI.

MY STRANGE DREAM.

For some time after retiring that night, I lay awake thinking, thinking. I had not bade Miss Emily good-bye. How sweet and lovely she was! And I—*I* had been rude to her.

At length drowsiness came over me and, for a few moments, I lost energy to think. Then I seemed to reawaken; about me there were din and confusion, the meaning and cause of which I could not explain. When the noise subsided, a great gloom gathered—a gloom of uncertainty. Into it I looked long in suspense. It seemed an eternity that I waited. I grew hot and almost stifled in the fever of anxiety which seemed to seize me. Something far away began to find form in the mysterious darkness; it approached, and I saw it to bear the

figure of a man. Some ghostly voice seemed
to whisper in my ear, "This is your fate,"
and I perceived, confronting me, my friend
Tyndall. Then flames shot up before my
eyes, Tyndall vanished, and I saw a burning
house. It was the Tracys'. Moans of anguish reached my ears, and Gertrude Tracy
and her father and mother were apparently
licked by tongues of flame as they fled from
the fire. I, on my part, was powerless to
render assistance. I tried to move, but felt
unable, for some unknown reason. A great
dread seized me. "Where was Emily? She
whom I loved ; where was she?"

Then the scene shifted. I was aboard a
ship and far out at sea. A dense fog hung
round about and close down over the water;
a melancholy pervaded all things. Several
muffled passengers, pacing the deck, looked
strangely unreal, through the mist. One of
the passengers drew near me, and I recognized in her figure and bearing some one I
had known. She was attired in deep mourn-
ing ; as she passed directly by me, our eyes
met. It was Emily Tracy! But she looked

at me without a sign of recognition in her face, and hurried on and disappeared. I was overcome with anguish.

The fog grew denser as I groped my way about the vessel, endeavoring to find Emily. Suddenly I seemed to see her again; and this time she smiled sadly at me, but I felt happy. Then terror struck my heart, for she seemed fading away into the fog beyond the vessel. In desperation I sprang overboard. Here my senses left me, and I knew no more.

At length I felt myself dreamily reawakening. And now I was no longer at sea, but, strange to relate, on land and near a railroad, for I heard the rumble of a fast approaching train. Footsteps sounded back of me: I turned, and perceived the lumbering figure of the misshapen man. He was pursuing some one, and that some one was Dooner; as the latter dashed past me, I saw his face. It was ashen white, and he trembled and looked terrified. An awful voice called after him :—

"Ef I catch yew I'll kill yew!"

It was the misshapen man who called.

"And if you *don't* catch me I'll tell the police about your murder. I'll get you hung!"

"It's a race fer life!" cried the misshapen man, and he madly ran on.

Now Dooner was crossing the railroad track; a woman suddenly appeared near by. She was very beautiful, and she stared wildly after Dooner.

"Avenge my daughter," she cried, "avenge my daughter!"

"He will die fer his brutality!" answered the misshapen man, furiously.

It flashed across me that the woman was the wife of the pursuer. The latter now espied me, for he called,

"Catch him fer me, catch him! Ef we let him go, *yew* will live ter rue the day. Yew'll never be safe until he's dead."

Then the speaker reached the tracks, and started to plunge across.—All this time the train had been drawing rapidly nearer.—When he was half-way over, the mighty engine seemed upon him, but to this he paid no heed. A whistle blew a terrific blast: my horror grew intense. I endeavored to rush out and save my chance acquaintance, the murderer, from his impending peril. But I found I could not move. I made a great effort, and, summoning all my powers, finally succeeded in dragging myself forward.

"I'm coming!" I called, but I could not see. My eyes were closed: I opened them. What might it mean? I felt dazed, for I found myself standing in the middle of my own room, with the sound from the whistle still ringing in my ears. Then it dawned upon me that I had been dreaming. The whistling came from a factory near-by; it was the morning signal calling men to work. " It is also calling me to work," thought I, whereupon I proceeded to don my things, feeling weary, and as though I had not slept a wink.

A little later, sauntering up the street towards my club, I found it impossible to shake off recollections of my disagreeable and all too vivid dream. Thoughts of it possessed me; indeed I felt an unaccountable dread lest something had gone wrong while I slept. When about to pass by Tyndall's office, I was prompted to stop in and ask him to breakfast with me. For I felt in such condition that I craved companionship.

Tyndall appeared unusually glad to see me, and his effusive greeting was comforting and welcome. He expressed surprise at my being about "at such an early hour."

He explained that he himself had "only just got up, preparatory to taking a morning spin on the wheel before beginning the day's labors."

No, he had not breakfasted. He accepted my invitation, so we repaired to the club.

During our repast the conversation, through no fault of mine, became of a personal nature. In fact, it concerned me particularly. Tyndall was very sympathetic and tried to get me to talk of myself. He asked me about my money affairs: if I had "any surplus lying idle" which I "might care to invest in a splendid enterprise?"

I naturally replied to this question by asking another: "What is the enterprise?"

"This," my friend said. "Of course, you know of Madeira?"

I started in surprise. "Yes," I answered.

"Halloo," exclaimed my friend, and then he leaned towards me and looked me fixedly in the eyes. Tyndall had a habit of doing this, and I never liked it. I have heretofore stated that he claimed to be something of a hypnotist. Though I did not then have faith in such imaginary power, I have since had good reason to change my belief. Whenever Tyndall looked at me as I have just described I always met his gaze, for I will not permit any man to make me drop my eyes. In Tyndall's stare there was the essence of self-possession. I have frequently seen him "look a man out of countenance," and then, in an off-hand manner, address some remark to the innocent victim which would startle, and set him to wondering. When Tyndall took his eyes from me I felt a little strangely. He seemed to have pierced my mind with his keen and apparently abnormally developed vision.

"I did not know that you kept important

matters from a friend," he said casually, but in a slightly injured tone. " You never told me that your father died in Madeira."

I must have started, for I know that I jarred the table, upsetting several things thereon. But of my discomposure my friend took no notice. He cleverly turned the *mal-a-propos* subject into that of his scheme, and soon, in spite of myself, I became his attentive listener.

" Madeira," he said, " is one of the greatest lace and embroidery manufacturing centers in the world. Hundreds of young women spend their lives at lace-making, and they are experts in the art. England recognizes this fact : her importations of Madeira lace are very large. Still, the output of lace in and about Funchal is enormous, and the demand is less by 80 per cent. than the supply."

Now this topic doubtless makes very uninteresting reading, and, as my thoughts had been striving to solve other and to me more immediately serious problems, I should myself have been restless and anxious to get away. Strangely, however, such was not the case. While Tyndall talked to me he never for an instant took his eyes from mine. Thus he controlled my entire attention, and he interested me, in spite of myself.

"Now," he said, "you have lots of money, and the entire control of it. Why, instead of dabbling occasionally down the street in stocks and bonds, don't you invest it, or the greater portion of it, in some business, and then start in at the head of that business, with a man as manager, who knows all the ropes, and make a big success and name for yourself? You ought to do this before you marry, for *after* a man marries, if he is the right sort like you, he wants to devote his time to his wife; hence he finds no time for his ambition or for active life, especially this is the case when he has money and can afford to loaf. Now here is an opportunity for you to distinguish yourself. I have given to the matter long and careful study, and I know all the details connected with it. Organize a company for the purpose of importing for sale in this country Madeiran lace and embroidery. The

United States is the field for the disposal of
Madeira's unexcelled product ; and, were the
new business properly handled, an enormous
market for these goods could be found in
this country within a year after starting.
Should you take the thing up, you would
want to do it in the right way, or, on the
other hand, not at all. To be frank, it would
take a large capital."

My friend paused, as if to test my interest :
I begged him to proceed. He accordingly
did so, and he talked on with such earnestness, and to such purpose, that he roused
my enthusiasm. He showed me clearly that
he knew a great deal about importing and
exporting, and also about the manufacture
of the articles in question, out in Madeira.
And, in the end, I found myself promising
to look into the matter. He then coolly requested that I loan him some money, sufficient to take him to Madeira, where he might
investigate matters for me.

His eyes glowed like live coals, and seemed
to burn my sight with their fire, as he awaited
my reply. I shook off a strange feeling of
numbness which was creeping over my con-

centrated thoughts, and abruptly turned the subject of the conversation. At this action Tyndall appeared nettled. He looked away from me for a few moments; after which he returned his gaze, and said sharply :—

"So you left your dear friends the Tracys in a huff last night?"

For the instant I was dumfounded at Tyndall's impudence, and also at his perspicacity. I asked him angrily why he should inquire into a subject which in no way concerned him.

He replied,

"My dear boy, I know some things without being told; and I concluded, when you first dropped in on me this morning, that you had had a misunderstanding with Miss Tracy. Otherwise, how could you have been so gloomy? Was it bad dreams?"

Here I was again surprised. Tyndall had a way of "hitting the nail on the head" that I did not like. But now, quick as a flash. my versatile acquaintance began the recounting of a funny story: when I left him a few minutes later my good humor had in a measure returned.

CHAPTER VII.

THE DEATH OF THE MURDERER.

I HAD bought the *Press;* but I could not read it, for thoughts of my dream recurred vividly to me. I sat peering listlessly out of the car window until I arrived at my destination. Then I set off for the house of the misshapen man, and soon reached his door.

The nurse answered my summons, and on my inquiring as to whether her patient's father was within, she replied in the negative. She further volunteered the statement that he had left the house about daybreak, and had not since put in an appearance.

When would he return?

She did not know; would I wait? She was not cognizant of his whereabouts, that she might direct me. No, I would not wait.

As I turned the corner from the alley

6

into the main street I almost collided with Tracy's coachman.

"Good marnin', sor," he said, stepping out of my way.

I replied to his salutation, and asked if the family were well and at home.

"They're all right, sor," he answered, "though there be them thot ain't." (This he said looking insolently knowing).

"They be in, sor, too, up to the place, though they bein't at home."

Concluding with which he turned upon his heel and walked away. I did not call him back to reprimand him for his impertinence. I had other and more important matters on hand. Foolish though it may seem, I felt greatly relieved now that I had learned, though from so rude an informant, of the Tracys' welfare: their house had not burned, as in my dream.

And now, where to find the murderer? This was my next thought. Pondering thus, I wandered along: oddly enough, I found myself returning in the direction of the railroad. Why not continue in this direction then? Not knowing *where* to look, was I not as likely to find him, for whom I had come in search, there as elsewhere?

Along the road I asked several persons I met if they had seen Tom Ugly-Face: thus he was known. The last individual I questioned was a boy who was passing me, breathless in haste and in excitement.

"Where's Tom Ugly-Face!" he shouted, repeating my question. "Why, you're behind de times, mister! Come along wid me an' I'll show him to you. He was run into and killed by a train dis morning, and dey've just brought in his corpse. Dey located it in a corn-field where de engyne's cow-catcher t'rowed it."

I fairly staggered at this startling news. "Take me to where he is," was all I could say, for I felt as though I were again in my dream. Indeed it appeared the natural sequence to my dream.

At my side skipped the lad; and I was recalled from a sort of lethargy by his question, which struck me as rather apt, in that he drew his inference from the manner in which the news of the misshapen man's demise had affected me :—

" Are you one of his folks ?" he queried cautiously.

Seeing the humorous side to this idea, I could not resist the temptation to encourage such a belief in the mind of my young guide.

We shortly reached the station, where we found a noisy, curious crowd collected. The people covered the platform about the station; they all seemed imbued with that thirst for excitement which constitutes the governing passion of a hastily gathered street throng. I was preparing to force my way through the thickest cluster of bystanders when a boyish voice, near me, called loudly :—

" Here's Tom Ugly-Face's brother; make room for him !"

Of course I looked about to see the individual thus announced. But I observed that all eyes were centered on me. For the moment I was bewildered. I saw that my youthful guide was at my elbow, and as he looked anxiously up into my face, it dawned upon me that my joke on him had turned into a larger joke upon myself.

It was an ordeal to explain to this assemblage that I was not " one of the folks." I felt obliged to do this, however. Then, as the people, having made a way for me, had not yet closed up their ranks, I quickly edged my way towards the spot where the body of the misshapen man lay. Several railroad officials stood at hand, and I could not obtain a very close view; that which I did see was sufficient to satisfy all my doubts, however. A dust-grimed and blood-spattered mass of flesh and clothing comprised all that remained of my unfortunate acquaintance. Life could not linger in so horribly contorted a form. And the strange part of the calamity's result was that the trunk and limbs were mangled, while the head and face remained undisturbed. Moreover, in death the face seemed to have taken, in some measure, those natural proportions which in life it lacked ; and there was a peculiar pathos in the expression which deeply touched me. Then I forgave the dead man that which I

knew of his life's crime. He had been unfortunate, and greatly wronged. And he
had been the avenger of my father's murder. *This* I should *never* forget; though I
profess to be a Christian, I inwardly thanked
his spirit, thereupon, from deep down in my
heart, and with such fervor that I felt that,
in some way, even then, he must surely be
aware of my gratitude. I determined to see
to it that the body received proper burial.
To strengthen this moral resolution, I addressed a policeman, and told him I meant
to take charge of the body.

At first he looked incredulous, but he
ended by consenting to let me have my way.

It took the responsibility from his shoulders of being officially obliged to look after
the repulsive corpse. I had an undertaker's
wagon called. To show my genuineness, I
paid a lump sum to the undertaker's repre-
sentative, the driver, for the removal of, and
proper attention to,. the remains. When
these had been taken away, and the crowd
had dispersed, I sat myself down upon a
vacant bench.

I had indeed placed myself in a novel position. I could not help recalling my dream: since, by some odd chance, my sleeping mind had witnessed the near approach of a catastrophe which now in reality had come to pass, I wondered if the rest of my dream would remain unrealized. Just then I felt that some one's gaze was upon me, and I lifted my eyes to see, standing before me, the disheveled and unkempt figure of a woman. This seemed like an apparition. But the woman, having caught my eye, looked long and steadily at me. Traces of a bygone beauty were apparent in her worn and haggard countenance; she was pale and trembling. She spoke, and her voice sounded cracked and far away :—

"My husband! He has been killed, and you have proved a friend in time of death. May the blessing of Almighty God fall upon you!"

The roots of my hair felt a tickling cold play among them; here was another actor from my dream. What had I done that I should be thus tormented? Then I became rational.

"Can I be of service to you, madam?" I inquired. "And is it indeed your husband who has been killed?"

"Thomas Griffith, my poor husband, is dead. I, his wretched wife, who should have died long ago in his stead, am left to mourn his loss." The unhappy woman burst into choking, tearless sobs.

I was glad she was not aware that I knew the story of her life. She nevertheless volunteered to me the information that she was about to return to her daughter and her home, and to undertake the duties of the widow and mother.

I asked her, as a test question, if she loved her daughter very much.

" Love her!" she cried. " No mother ever loved a child more than I love my daughter *now!* And oh, how she has suffered! and all through my neglect!" Here her voice lowered to a whisper, as she continued, to herself, "And to think that Rose is a mother now!"

This was all I heard for some moments, as my unexpected visitor mumbled inaudibly to herself. At length an expression came into her face such as had not been there before. Her eyes flashed; the color mounted to her faded cheeks. She sprang forward and seized my arm.

"Dooner," she moaned, "is the cause of it all."

"What has Dooner to do with it?" I asked.

She drew herself up proudly, and made answer :—

"He insulted my daughter. My husband, who saw him arrive at the Junction by an early morning train, chased him. Dooner was scared and ran up the track. I saw them coming from where I was a-sitting on a fence by the railroad up there" (pointing).

"When Dooner saw me he got worse scared, and crossed the track right in front of an up express.* Bad luck to him, he got across all right. But my husband tripped and fell on the track. And, oh my God! before I could run to him, the engine struck

* Train bound for New York.

him. It sent him up, up, into the air, and out of sight. At least out of *my* sight, for after that I didn't know any more. I must have fainted dead away and have fallen and rollen down the bank; for when I came to I was a-laying in a swampy place, where the railroad was away above me and up a hill."

The lamenting woman waved her arms in wild gesticulation. She began to sway from faintness, so that I thought she would fall. I stood up to hold her, but she motioned me away. Clutching a post, the contact with such support returned her her strength. Once more she drew herself erect, though slowly; and she let one hand rest upon the post as she again addressed me.

"When I got my wits about me and remembered what had happened, I almost swooned again. But I kept myself from a-going off, and I climbed up by the railroad tracks and started to hunt for my poor husband.

"The day must have been well started when I first came to, for the sun was high up. Well, I hunted and searched for the

longest while, round about the place where
the engine had thrown my poor man into the
air. I kept a-calling out 'Tom! Tom!' all
the time, but no voice answered. Then a
man came walking along the tracks. He
asked me what I was looking for. I told
him. 'You'll find the body up to the station; they've carried it there,' says he.
'Then he's dead?' I screamed at him. The
man looked solemn and nodded his head.
Then I sank down on my knees, and he told
me how he was sorry for me. 'Sorry!' says
I; 'I want no sympathy, thank you!' I got
up and left him, and came here to the station.
Still I couldn't find my husband's body; but
I learned what had become of it, and how
kind and charitable you had been. And I
had you pointed out to me; and here I am
before you, and to thank you—"

I interposed.

"I merely did my duty, madam; and, believe me, I feel deep gratitude to your husband for a service he once rendered me. In
life I have never repaid him for this service;
so permit me to do so now." I drew forth

my wallet, took out a fifty-dollar bill, and
tendered it to her. But she drew back,
and stiffly remarked,—

"I thank you, but I am not a beggar,
sir!"

"I see that plainly, and I had no thought
of offering this to you for yourself. It is for
your daughter and your little grandchild;
indeed, your daughter need never know how
you came by it."

"For my daughter and her little one!" the
woman said, passionately. "Oh, good gentleman, you are too kind, too kind! I shall
take the money, if it is for them. But no:
first, I must know of the service my husband
performed for you, and which you state is
unpaid for."

This was unexpected, and I felt my situation an embarrassing one. However, I haz-
arded a reply to this point-blank question.

"I beg that you press me no further on
this matter. The service was a *great* service.
And if you take me to be a gentleman, since
thus you called me, I trust that you will give
due credit to the word of a gentleman; I

assure you that this money is a trifle to me compared with the value of the service performed. Allusion to this service gives me pain, and I therefore request that you regard my feelings."

The woman looked at me keenly for a moment, as if to read my thoughts; then her gaze fell, and she said simply,—

"I accept the money, gracious gentleman, and I shall ever pray the good Lord to bless you for your kindness."

I have always disliked thanks, so I hastened to draw my conversation with Mrs. Griffith to a close. I told her I had made the arrangements for the interment of her husband, and that she need call but once upon the funeral director, and then only to make him a small payment which would be due after the burial.

The platform began to vibrate more and more until a heavy train rolled up to the station. I bade farewell to the poor widow, and clambered to the platform of the rear car, where I stood while the train got under way. Before turning a bend in the road, which would hide the depot from view, I could still see the widow of the misshapen man standing, looking after me; then, even as I saw her, she turned and walked away. And I judged she would return to her daughter.

PART II.

TRANQUIL was the water, the weather, balmy.
  I sailed the summer sea
In careless mood, until the skies grew stormy:
  And then, ah, woe was me!

A tempest wild arose. It broke, and, raging,
  Tossed my boat to and fro.
But back to the Isle of my childhood, changing,
  I swept, willing or no.

CHAPTER I.

AT NEWPORT.

I was to meet Miss Blumer at the Casino at half-past twelve o'clock. The Van Dennis's ball of the night previous had been a long affair. I had been obliged to remain until after daybreak, as young Van Dennis, a very good fellow, had especially requested me to stay and have a little chat with him and other friends when the rest of the guests had departed. I hadn't seen as much of Miss Blumer as I should have liked. She was always dancing whenever I wished to speak with her. This put me in a very bad humor. I am not a dancing man myself. A number of girls sat out dances with me; but Miss Blumer's manner had been most exasperating. The only time I succeeded in getting a word with her was previous to the last dance, before the grand march to supper.

7

On this occasion I had just bowed away her other attendant, and was in the act of taking his vacated seat beside her, when the orchestra struck up a waltz. Immediately, and as if by magic, three men presented themselves in a row before us. Each asked Miss Blumer if he might be her partner for the dance.

"I regret very much that I shall be obliged to refuse you all, as I have this dance engaged," she replied, inclining her head and smiling sweetly.

At this my heart beat faster within me, and I am sure my face reddened, for I felt conscious that Miss Blumer was refusing these men's attentions for my company. The men evidently thought so, for they scowled at me, and at one another, and then went away. But they were mistaken. I saw that, though Miss Blumer entertained me, she had a preoccupied manner. When on the point of remarking that "I felt highly honored in that she should wish to sit out a dance with a stupid such as I," an unexpected interruption occurred. The dance *had*

really been engaged, for the tardy partner
put in his appearance; Miss Blumer arose
and glided off with him into the maze of
dancers, smiling bewitchingly after me as
she disappeared in the throng. I hated that
fellow and resolved to show him an example
of my contempt whenever the opportunity
to do so might arise.

Well, I had been in Newport for about a
week; and, ever since my arrival, I had been
made tolerably miserable by the unaccountable actions of Miss Blumer. She was always
perplexing me, in spite of which I found myself constantly dancing attendance upon her,
only to be put off and to be rendered the
more perplexed by her. And now, even now,
I was going to meet her. I resolved that I
would ask her why she had left me at the
ball, to go off with another man. I felt that
she had no *right* to leave me as she had done.
For another man, too! Ha! it made me furious, violently furious, to think of it. Then
I laughed at myself. I laughed as I locked
my room door and took the key out, and I
laughed as I went downstairs.

"What's the joke?" inquired a familiar voice.

I looked up indignantly. It was Trotter, Bobby Trotter, the gay old beau. He was dressed in immaculate golf costume of enormous check pattern, and his spindly legs, below the knees, were incased in heavy stockings—not heavy enough, however, to conceal the thin appearance of his person.

"Which way are you going, Hall?" he asked, as I attempted to pass him.

"Don't know," I answered abruptly.

"Oh well, Hall, don't be impatient; haul me along with you." And he chuckled away at his stupid pun until his face became crimson. What was still more annoying, he linked arms with me, and accompanied me to the hotel office.

"Going out?"

"No."

"Well, then, come and hit one with me; here's the bar."

I answered that I did not care to drink so early, but that I intended getting a bite of something in the dining-room, before starting out. I had not yet breakfasted.

"Ah, well, I'm not finicky, so I'll be good-natured and come and have a cocktail in the lunch-room with you—I prefer the bar—while you're taking your late repast. *I* breakfasted *hours* ago."

I didn't care if he had. Trotter always nettled me, and still he unceasingly sought my company. Seated at the table, I ordered ham and eggs, and Trotter raised his monocle and squinted through it at me.

"Country fare," said he, "country fare. Why do you not order a little fois gras, buttered toast and a pint of Pontet Canet, if this is your déjeuner?"

He ordered his cocktail, and when it was brought in on a tray with my breakfast he remarked that he hoped the proximity of the ham and eggs had not hurt the flavor of his beverage. I made my meal a short one, for I was in a hurry to be off. By the time my companion had emptied his glass, I had finished my repast.

"Whither now?" asked Trotter.

"I'm going to the Casino to keep an engagement," I answered, rising from the table.

"Whom with, you naughty, naughty boy? A young lady, to be sure, I presume, and a mighty pretty one at that, if it is Miss Blumer?"

My cheeks grew hot; I felt like throwing something at the old dude.

"There, there, do not blush, do not blush. I knew it, you see. Indeed everybody knows it, deah boy. Mrs. Blumer says she is greatly pleased. I congratulate you upon your choice."

"Congratulate me upon what choice?" I blundered.

"Don't act like a fool, Hall. Own up like a man. When will the engagement be announced?"

I was angry, and must have shown it, for Trotter added,—

"There, there, don't be cross. I hate scenes. I apologize if I have offended you. It is common talk that you are engaged to Miss Blumer. I merely wished to ask you, as a friend, if it is true?"

"Miss Blumer has not so honored me," I replied, "and I can tell you there is no truth in such report."

"All right, deah boy, all right. Enough's enough, and we have spoken enough on this subject, I see. Now, I think, we'll part company, if you do not object, for I know of some chaps who are going over to the links to have a game, and I think I shall join them."

Of course I did not object.

"*Au revoir* but not good-bye," Trotter sang out as he strode away.

I regretted that it was *not* good-bye to him. And I made my way to the Casino. Here I found Miss Blumer strolling before the building in company with a couple of men. She did not observe my approach, and my heart beat quickly as I looked at her, for she was very beautiful. I am an *ignoramus* on the subject of woman's dress, but I could not help observing how faultlessly Miss Blumer was attired. In figure and bearing she was tall and stately. She had black hair that she wore at the back of her shapely head, in a coil, through which was thrust a chased gold poniard; in the hilt of the poniard glittered a single, large emerald. This fashion of hair-dress was a characteristic; she never varied it. Now she—whose attention had thus far apparently been engrossed, listening to a recital of one of the men— looked up. Her dark eyes sparkled as they met the sun's rays, and she nodded to me and quickened her pace. I had been looking but at her; as I came up to the trio, imagine my intense surprise to find that one was Tyndall.

"I ran up to see how you were getting along," he said casually, and looking me coolly in the eye. Then he cast a rapid glance full of meaning towards the young lady, which she (fortunately, I thought) did not observe. At this ungallant conduct I burned inwardly with rage. I should give Tyndall a piece of my mind when I had him by himself. The other man was Miss Blumer's waltz partner of the night before. Now both men lifted their hats to Miss Blumer and took their departure. Tyndall did not so much as give me a glance as he strolled away.

"Let us take a walk along the bluff; I do so love to watch the breakers!" said Miss Blumer.

We accordingly turned our way seaward.

"What brought Tyndall up here, do you know?" I asked.

"Doctor Tyndall? He came to see me. What do *you* think?" Miss Blumer replied. Then she watched me languidly, through half-closed eyes, as if to study the effect her words might have upon me. I judge I am a poor hand at concealing my feelings. I invariably remember a little too late that my face is an index to my thoughts, through its expression.

Miss Blumer laughed :—

"Why, you droll fellow; I do believe you are jealous of any attention to me other than your own." Then her eyelids drooped, and she became silent and pensive.

I spoke up heatedly,—

"Indeed I am jealous, jealous of everybody you have anything to do with. Do you not care for me, just a little bit?"

"Mr. Hall, you know I like you—I count you among my dearest friends."

"Oh pshaw! Friends! you always put me off that way."

"Why, Mr. Hall, what do you mean? I am afraid I do not understand you."

"I mean——"

"Yes?"

"I mean——"

"Yes?"

Well, why couldn't I say what I meant? Whenever my opportunity came to tell Miss Blumer of my love for her, I found I had not the power. I was agitated, but I could not think of a fitting way to introduce the subject of my heart's desire. As Miss Blumer said nothing to relieve my embarrassment, and as she waited to hear me out, I felt that I must say something without further delay, so I stammered,—

"I mean that I want to be the only one to pay you attention."

Miss Blumer turned and, looking me full in the face, said,—

"Oh, I'm tired; let's go back to the Casino and get an ice."

Now, this is an example of the treatment which I was constantly receiving from Miss Blumer. I could not understand why she

would make an appointment with me to go
upon a walk or an excursion, and then,
when we had started, would suddenly appear bored and wish to turn back. This
time I pleaded with the perverse young
lady, for it made me desperate to be thus
trifled with. But, having once set her mind
on returning, nothing that I could say would
cause her to alter her course. So neither of
us was in a very amiable mood, as we re-
traced our steps.

On the way up the Casino walk Tyndall
met us. This time his manners were fault-
less. He raised his hat gracefully to Miss
Blumer and greeted her politely. Then he
addressed me in a hearty, sincere, and open
fashion, telling me that he was delighted to
see me. He continued to make himself
agreeable, and begged Miss Blumer that he
might accompany us. Permission granted,
we strolled along. Tyndall was jolly and
entertaining, and he recounted a number of
amusing anecdotes. As I regained my good
humor I felt that it might be as well that
Miss Blumer had insisted upon turning back.

Perhaps she really did not entertain the feelings for me that I had hoped to have aroused in her. I decided to abide the proper time, and to curb my impatience.

We went onto the porch of the Casino and chose a small table, where we seated ourselves and ordered some refreshments.

"Oh, Mr. Hall," said Miss Blumer, clapping her daintily gloved hands, "I have heard all about your great business plan and I heartily approve of it. I do think that every man ought to do something, whether he be rich or poor. And it is so fine that you want to make a name for yourself. Put me down for one of your prospective customers of Madeira lace. I hear it is beautiful."

I looked at Tyndall inquiringly, and he nodded and smiled. So I said to Miss Blumer,—

"I should have told you this before, but *I* had regarded it as a business secret."

Here Tyndall interrupted,—

"It is a business secret, but you surely do not object to Miss Blumer's knowing?"

I felt my face turn red, and I stammered,—
"Of course not."

Then I went on to tell Miss Blumer that
Tyndall and I had discussed the matter but
once together, and that no steps were as yet
contemplated for the taking up of the project.

Miss Blumer expressed her disappointment
at this information, and she said,—

"Oh, but you surely will go into such a
splendid enterprise? Mr. Tyndall has told
me all about it, and if you wish to please
me, go into it."

I thanked Miss Blumer for her interest in
me, and told her that I now felt I must
assuredly show my appreciation of such a
compliment by taking the matter up. It
made me intensely happy to think that *she*
cared what I did.

A number of friends now joined us, so we
all went off to the links to have a game before dinner. It was evening ere I succeeded
in getting word in private with Tyndall.

"*She* wishes that I go into the business,"
was my chief thought.

Tyndall and I sat together discussing

business topics until a late hour; and, when we retired, he took a room next to mine, at the Cliff House. The day following was to witness a magnificent regatta between three of the fastest sailing boats afloat. It promised to be *the* event of the late season. I had been invited to view the marine spectacle from the deck of the Van Dennis' yacht. Miss Blumer and her mother would also be among the guests. A note had just been brought to my room from Van Dennis, giving me permission to bring my friend Tyndall.

I was aroused at daybreak by a knocking at my door, which I opened to find Tyndall, dressed, and wanting me to go out with him to see the sun rise.

"What an energetic chap you are!" I said. "Seeing it's you, I'll go." I guessed, and rightly, that the sunrise was a pretext of Tyndall's to get me out, in order that he, in his impatience, might continue his talk on business matters. We went down to the water and had a look at the yachts which had come in to be present at the regatta. The sky was still flooded with golden light, for

the sun was not yet high, and there were
fleecy clouds that caught its slanting rays.
Many yachts lay at their moorings, and
aboard them uniformed sailors were busily
engaged in scrubbing decks, hoisting colors,
and getting things in proper readiness for
the day's festivities.

My spirits rose, and I felt thrilled with
enthusiasm at the prospect. A barefooted
urchin passed near us crying out, "Morning papers!"

I hailed him and asked if he had any Philadelphia papers. He looked scornfully up at
me and replied,—

"Never have 'em, sir; you can't git Philadelphia newspapers nowheres 'round here."

"Have you the New York *Times*, then?"
I inquired.

"To-day's New York papers haven't come
in yet."

"Well, then, what have you?"

"Got the Pawtucket and Providence
papers, sir."

"Give me the Providence *Journal*," I said.
Tyndall bought a Pawtucket *Post*.

We pocketed the morning news, and set off on our return to the hotel. The early outing had made us very hungry. We sat down to breakfast prepared to do full justice to what might be set before us.

When the waiter had duly filled our goblets with ice water and had taken orders, we unfolded our newspapers for brief perusal. As was his custom, Tyndall looked first to the financial news. I noticed this and then turned my attention to the *Journal's* first page. I always begin a paper by glancing through its dispatch columns. First the headings :—

" Foreign News ;" " The London Letter ;" " Burned Alive;" "Japan again Victorious;" "To-day's Regatta."

" Foreign News ;" I'll read that later.

" The London Letter ;" that can wait.

" Burned Alive;" ah—hem! that sounds exciting.

BURNED ALIVE!

Frightful Fate of a Prominent Author and his Family.

Special to the JOURNAL.

HOLMESBURG, PA., August 19.

One of the most terrible fires ever known in this locality took place to-night.

The residence of Stedman Tracy, the well-known author, was hidden in the midst of great, tree-grown, ancestral grounds; and its burning was only discovered when flames shot high into the air and the fire was well under way. In fact when the first of the crowd attracted by the blaze did arrive on the scene of the disaster they were too late to render assistance to the unfortunate occupants, for a mass of charred and flickering ruins was all that remained of the building.

And the firemen, too, who came about this time, are now working to find the bodies of the victims.

A woman in the service of the Tracys made her escape, and states that she occupied a room on the ground floor, and that the fire started somewhere in the story above, in the sleeping apartments.

The hour was well on to midnight—and the Tracys had all retired early—when the woman awoke to a sense that she was surrounded by smoke and flame. She barely managed to save her own life. It is feared that not one of the family escaped, but that all perished within the burning walls—

I could read no more. My sight dimmed, and I trembled violently. It took all my strength to keep myself from falling upon the floor. Not a word could I say, but when Tyndall looked at me he told me I was pale as a ghost. He became greatly concerned, and pressed me to tell what ailed me. To him I paid no heed. Rising unsteadily from the table, I left the dining room. It was difficult for me to walk. My head felt light, and objects waved before my eyes.

"My dream," I thought; "my dream: it has come true."

I was conscious of being regarded curiously as I passed along the hall to the staircase. I ascended to my bedchamber, entered, and slammed the door. Tyndall had followed me. His voice came from without :—

"Let me in. Let me know your trouble!"

I told him to leave me to myself for a little while, stating that I might join him later. Anything to get rid of him and of *every one* for a few moments. Tyndall went away. I flung myself upon the bed, and, though it

may have been unmanly, I burst into tears.
Now I knew whom I loved. I loved Emily
Tracy. I always had loved her, it seemed;
and yet I had only just discovered it. I
tore my hair, and raved in the madness of
despair.

"Emily, Emily, Emily!"

I pulled at the features of my face, and
contorted myself, as in a fit.

Oh, what a fool I was! Why had I left
Philadelphia? Had not my dream come as
a prediction to me, and had I not awakened
to immediately realize part of it? I felt as
though guilty of some dreadful crime.

"All dead!" I sobbed in my misery. "All
dead, and they perished as in my dream.
Why did I not warn them in time? Or
why, at least, did not I, myself, take heed
from the vivid happenings of my dream? I
should have watched and waited."

A feeling seized me that I was the victim
of delusion:—

It could not be that the Tracys' house had
really burned, and that my love had been
lost. I still grasped the paper containing

the dread report. I smoothed it out. The heading, "Burned Alive," was all that I could see.

"Sensational title. What if the report is false? It may be. It is!" I almost shouted. Then I grew calmer. I began to reason: "The report may be true in part. The dispatch was evidently received quite late and but shortly before this paper went to press, for the statement is that the fire did not occur until about twelve o'clock last night. After all, though the paper says, 'It is feared that not one of the family escaped,' it may not be so."

My memory brought before me handsome, dashing Miss Gertrude: I could not believe her dead. I thought of kind Mr. Tracy, and of sweet Mrs. Tracy. Could it be possible that they were no more?

My pulses throbbed, and I grew hot and cold alternately, in the intensity of my feelings. I clung in recollection to the people with whom I associated so many past joys and true happinesses. Thoughts of my dream again recurred to me. "Emily still lives," I told myself, "for she survived the fire in my dream."

Oh idle laggard and wretched mope that I felt myself to be! I beat my chest and sprang to my feet. Inactive no longer should I be. "Find Emily Tracy!" This was now my resolve. I rushed about the room like a madman, collecting my clothes and various belongings, and tossing them, pellmell, into my steamer trunk. Not once did I think of Miss Blumer. Soon ready for departure, I descended to the hotel office. The bus was at the door; and I found myself just in time to catch the morning boat and to make connection with a through train to New York.

At the wharf Tyndall met me. He said he was awaiting my arrival. Having noted that I had been disturbed by something in the morning paper, and having failed to learn from me the cause of my distemper, he had searched carefully through his own newspaper. He found a dispatch about the Tracy disaster and guessed that this it was which affected me. The boat was about to leave; Tyndall expressed deep sympathy for me and wished me a safe journey and good fortune. I asked him to make my excuses to the Van Dennises for my non-attendance at the yachting party. He said he would do so; he made no reference to either Mrs. Blumer or her daughter. In this I appreciated his good sense. Tyndall and I parted, though, as I stepped aboard, he called to me :—

"I shall follow you to Philadelphia in a couple of days. I would go with you now but that I fear you may not wish my companionship."

CHAPTER II.

SHE WHOM I LOVE.

SUFFICE it to say, in referring to my journey to Philadelphia by way of New York, that I passed the time in a fever of anxiety. When the express from Jersey City whizzed by Holmesburg Junction, I felt it hard to restrain myself from jumping from my car. At Germantown Junction the panting engine slowed, and came to a momentary standstill. I alighted, in the hope of catching a way-train back to Holmesburg; in this I was not disappointed.

Never shall I forget the smallest incident connected with that eventful night. Since then I have been a changed man: a man graver, a man sadder.

I ran the entire distance from the depot at Holmesburg Junction to the home of the late misshapen man. The Griffith woman met me in the doorway; she was standing

there when I came up. By the light of a
street lamp across the way, she looked even
more ghastly than when I had last seen her,
and in her face I seemed to read the tale of
an awful and more recent catastrophe than
the death of her husband. She greeted me
with an outstretched, trembling hand, and
for the space of a full minute, though her
lips moved, she was unable to utter a sound.
Did I read her thoughts?

"Tell me the worst!" I cried. "What is
it?"

Still she did not speak, and I felt in a tor-
ment of suspense.

"The Tracys!" I gasped. "Tell me!"

My heart stopped beating; heavy drops
of sweat blurred my sight. Was it a fate
that confronted me? I listened to a voice,
broken and weary :—

"Such a wicked fire never burned before!
The good folks died in their beds. And
poor, dear Miss Emily!"

"What?" I asked, choking, as I seized
my informant's arm and looked earnestly
into her face.

"She's the only one alive."

"Alive!" I ejaculated, "alive! I thank Heaven. But is she uninjured?"

For a brief space there was no answer; I grew embarrassed under a gaze, quizzical and then comprehensive, of Mrs. Griffith's. At length she said,—

"Not a hair of Miss Emily's head was burned. Miss Gertrude rescued her, instead of saving herself."

"Is Miss Gertrude dead?"

"She died from the effects of her burns, early this morning. She was buried to-night, about sundown. It is Miss Emily now I pity most, for her poor soul is wrung with sorrow, and she pleads and longs to die."

"Where is she?" I asked, unable to say more, as I leaned against the doorway, weak from the intensity of my feelings.

"At Doctor Townsend's; where she was taken directly she was saved, from burning, by her sister."

"And did Miss Gertrude really rescue her at the risk of her own life?"

By way of reply Mrs. Griffith handed me a newspaper. It was that evening's Philadelphia *Bulletin*.

"Read for yourself; there's a full account, and better than I can give you," she said.

My eyes fastened upon the column to which she pointed. It was on the front page, and the article was headed by a double-column picture entitled, "The Late Miss Gertrude Tracy; A Noble Heroine." Mrs. Griffith invited me into her dwelling, but I declined. I crossed the alley to the street lamp, and by its dim light hastily scanned the detailed account of the fire. Then I returned the paper to Mrs. Griffith and, bidding her "good-night," hurried to Dr. Townsend's house.

The doctor answered the door in person. He looked very grave, and I could see that he was deeply afflicted. He had been a close and dear friend to Mr. Tracy and his family. Though I had never before met Dr. Townsend I knew him by reputation to be an excellent physician and a man of fine character. Briefly introducing myself to him as a

friend of the Tracys, I asked to see Miss
Emily.

He stated that many friends had been there
that day, but that under no circumstances
would he sanction *anybody's* seeing the
young lady for at least a fortnight. She
was under the care of a trained nurse, and
suffering from an acute attack of nervous
prostration.

Not wishing to detain the doctor too long,
I left him my sympathy, and departed.
Next, visiting the scene of the late disastrous conflagration, the first sight of the
charred ruins only added to my sickening
sorrow. With a heavy heart I returned to
town.

*   *   *   *   *   *   *   *

A few days later the will of the late Mr.
Tracy was published. Miss Emily fell heir-
ess to the entire estate, valued at some
$250,000. The old Tracy homestead was put
up at auction, and, to my great surprise, the
purchaser was Tyndall. He had just returned
to Philadelphia. I called on him : I could
not understand what my friend should wish

with a country place. Furthermore, I knew that he possessed little or no money of his own. He had been expecting to see me. He said he was not surprised at my wonder and curiosity regarding his purchase. He laughed at me as he explained that he merely acted as an agent in the matter. He had bought the place for some one else, but the name of that some one he declined to divulge. I could not help being provoked at this secrecy from me. Still I then thought that, as the transaction did not directly concern me, it was no business of mine to press an unwelcome question.

I could not long remain absent from the vicinity of the girl I loved. I journeyed to Holmesburg about every twenty-four hours for the simple satisfaction of hearing Dr. Townsend's latest report on the condition of his patient. Upon such visits I rarely saw the doctor himself, though he always left word with the maid at the door. Miss Emily's illness was long and tedious.

It was after I had called at Dr. Townsend's a number of times, and when he again answered the door in person, that I took occasion to make an apology for bothering him so frequently. The doctor smiled kindly, and answered,—

"I know of but one other young man who calls so persistently, inquiring after Miss Tracy; like yourself, he is a stranger to me."

It seems needless to state that this remark aroused my violent jealousy. Dr. Townsend was a kindly, elderly man. I questioned him closely concerning the appearance of my rival visitor. He would leave no name at the doctor's. On learning his description I was startled: it was that of Tyndall. I bade good-day to the doctor and returned to the city.

Tyndall was as usual in his office when I rushed in upon him. I demanded to know if he had been out to Holmesburg recently.

He looked surprised, and asked in turn if anything were the matter.

"Most certainly something *is* the matter," I answered. "You have been out to Holmesburg every day, have you not?"

"I have not," Tyndall quietly replied. Then his eyes shone fiercely, and he leaned forward in his office chair and remarked curtly: "But what if I had? Should I have to ask your permission?"

To this there appeared no reply that I might suitably make. Tyndall had, figuratively speaking, cornered me. He said he had *not* been to Holmesburg, so I decided to take his word. If the caller described by Dr. Townsend was not Tyndall, then whom might he be? This I would discover. When we resumed conversation on an amicable basis, Tyndall said,—

"If you very much want to know whether I have been out to Holmesburg, I will tell you that I *have* been there once; it was when I bought that Tracy property."

I spoke no more on the subject, but I resolved to change the hour of my trip to Holmesburg, that I might perchance encounter my rival visitor. The following evening I boarded a way-train for the Junction. When I had seated myself I looked up: Tyndall was approaching through the

car. Now I seemed for once to have the
best of him. He started as I called out,—

"Where are you going?"

For the moment I felt sure I had disconcerted him. But he came forward and
greeted me cordially.

"This is luck," he said; "I hope you are
going near my destination, which to-night is
Holmesburg. I am running out to have a
look at the Tracy property, still mine *pro
tempore*."

I told Tyndall that I was bound for the
same place whither he was going. At the
depot we parted.

Arriving before the doctor's door I tapped
his old-fashioned knocker, as ordinarily. The
doctor was not at home. He had gone away
for an absence of several days, the maid in-
formed me.

"How was Miss Tracy?"

"Oh, better, but mournful-like. Her aunt
called for her this morning, and took her
away."

"Away?" I asked, "Where?"

The servant could not tell me.

"Is she not coming back?"

"No, sir," the woman replied decisively.

When, at the depot, I again met Tyndall, he noted immediately that something was wrong with me. He had withheld his confidence from me, however, so I resolved to tell him nothing of my present affairs. It was in vain that he questioned me.

I shall not dwell upon the events of the long-drawn days during which I made various and unsuccessful attempts at discovering the whereabouts of her whom I loved. Suffice it to say that I eventually succeeded: Miss Tracy had gone to the home of her aunt in Chicago. I called to see Tyndall before my departure west; but his office was closed, and he was absent from town.

During my westward journey I occupied my time with the reading of a couple of Mr. Tracy's latest books. On arriving in Chicago I went directly to the Auditorium Hotel, where I engaged a room; and then I set out to find Miss Emily. Her aunt's residence was situated on Michigan Avenue near Twelfth Street. A short ride in the cab

took me thither. The driver knew Miss
Stanley's house. He said to me,—

"She is one of the most prominent ladies
in Chicago."

The dwelling of Miss Emily's aunt was
assuredly a magnificent building. To my
chagrin, it was closed. I applied to a next-
door neighbor for information.

Miss Stanley had left the city for an extended tour in Europe.

"When did she depart?"

"About four days ago."

I almost lost my self-control. Here I had
come out to Chicago while Emily had gone
to New York. In my eagerness, I had un-
wittingly been journeying away from her.
As my latest informant could furnish me with
no further particulars, I resumed my seat in
the cab, and drove to the nearest post-office.
Miss Stanley had left directions to have her
mail forwarded in care of Messrs. Brown
Brothers, London. This was all the satisfaction I had got by coming west.

I returned to my hotel, downcast and dis-
heartened. Even yet Emily might be in

New York. But it would take me twenty-
four hours to reach there should I start immediately, and she might have sailed for
Europe ere I arrived. I ordered luncheon,
but, when it was served, found that I had
no appetite. I ate little or nothing. The
eastbound train for New York did not leave
until evening. The afternoon remained to
me to spend in Chicago *nolens volens.*

I sauntered to the office, where I took up
the hotel register and looked over the names
of the most recent arrivals. I could hardly
believe my eyes when they fell upon the
familiar signature of James Brown Tyndall.

" Is he here?" I asked the clerk, reversing
the signature book and pointing to the name
of the doctor.

" Don't you see it for yourself, sir?" replied the clerk testily. " He came last evening."

I scowled at the fellow for his rudeness.
But this was *perplexing.* I seated myself in
a chair facing a large window. Putting on
my " thinking cap" and gazing moodily out
into the street, I became oblivious of all im-

mediate surroundings. So Tyndall was in
Chicago. What did his presence here mean?
Could it have anything to do with Miss
Tracy? Why such a thought as this occurred to me I do not know. Nevertheless, I
wondered, and as I wondered I grew angered
and agitated. "Whatever is his business
here," I assured myself, "I am the last person in the world he will expect to meet!"
Hardly had I thought this when a hand was
clapped heavily upon my shoulder.

I sprang up in wrath, which turned to surprise when I found myself confronted with
the very man of whom I had been thinking.

His first words disconcerted me:

"You are the person I have been waiting
for. Though I must say I expected to have
had the pleasure of your company on my way
out here."

"Look here, Jim," I said, "how on earth
did you know I was coming to Chicago, and
what has brought you here yourself?"

"I came out on a matter of business which
is now completed. So far as knowing about
you is concerned, I may as well tell you that

I know your little secret. Have you seen Miss Tracy?"

I turned quickly upon him.

"Now I want to know from you exactly what you know of Miss Tracy?"

Tyndall shrugged his shoulders, and replied without hesitation,—

"Why, old boy, don't I know you well enough to be aware of your flirtation? Besides, I belong to a medical society of which Dr. Townsend is a member. I heard in a roundabout way that Miss Tracy removed to this city since her misfortune, and is now living here with some relative, whose name I forget. A friend of mine told me that you had been to Holmesburg a couple of times, and had sent flowers and all those sorts of things out there. Now, to whom could you be sending floral tributes in Holmesburg save to Miss Tracy? A great time you had deciding between her and Miss Blumer! Didn't you tell me why you left Newport?"

I acknowledged to Tyndall that he was right in his conjecture. He then continued,—

"I suppose you have been dancing attend-

ance upon your lady ever since your arrival
out here this morning. If you have just
come from seeing her now, she must have
refused you, for I never saw any one look
more dejected."

It maddened me to hear Tyndall talk in
this way, and I abruptly turned the conversation.

"When do you return?" I said, in a tone
rather sterner than the question in itself required.

Tyndall observed my annoyance, and he
made no further reference to any subject
which was not agreeable.

We spent the remainder of the afternoon
seeing the sights of the city. Together we
took the evening train for home.

CHAPTER III.

IN SOCIETY'S WHIRL.

ABOUT a week had elapsed since my return from the West. I had gone to New York only to find that I arrived there too late. Miss Emily's and Miss Stanley's names appeared on the passenger list of the steamship Augusta Victoria: this vessel had sailed from New York on the morning of my arrival in Chicago. I discovered these facts by consulting the shipping news in the back files of the New York papers. At the office of the Hamburg-American Line, I ascertained that the passengers in whose movements I was interested were booked to land at Cherbourg, France. Such information helped me but little, however. Cherbourg is a port that offers quick access to Paris: the great majority of travellers landing at Cherbourg are bound for the French me-

tropolis, and do not linger at the quaint sea-
coast town.

Considering the little I yet know of Miss
Tracy's foreign destination, I had deemed
it would be unwise immediately to follow
her across the seas. I might have another
fruitless search for her. I immediately wrote
to Miss Stanley's London bankers, and, by
the same post, mailed a letter to Emily. In
the first writing I asked what Miss Stanley's
exact address might be a month ahead, as
nearly as her bankers could tell.

I had been a long time in preparing that
which I wrote in the second-mentioned letter.
It was to the girl whom I wished to make
my wife; whether she answered me or no, i
should ever love but her. It had been a difficult undertaking to put into words feelings
and longings that came from my heart's
depths. The subject required delicacy of
expression. And how many sheets of paper
I spoiled in the labor of composition I shall
not say. Neither shall I enter into detail
regarding the letter I finally succeeded in
penning to my satisfaction, and sent. Per-

haps, for the sake of the thread of the story, however, I should give my reader some *idea* of its general drift. I realize that subsequent events were largely brought about by this writing.

To begin with, I told Miss Tracy of my heartfelt sympathy with her in her grief and bereavement. I craved her pardon and offered every apology for the abrupt manner in which I had last left her. I begged that she would permit me to follow and meet her, wherever she might be, abroad. I told her, that I did not care to live unless she would forgive and let me see her once again. And so I sent this letter on its way to her. For the present there was nothing left for me to do but wait. So I returned to Philadelphia.

People were coming back to the fashionable quarters of town. I felt constrained to go about a little. Forced inactivity and suspense weighed heavily upon me. I needed diversion. The opening entertainment of the season was about to be given by two very good friends of mine, the Duanes, a rich young couple, recently married. Duane asked me to come early; so, when the evening for the dance arrived, I did so—though without availing myself of Mrs. Duane's dinner invitation.

It was rumored that Mrs. Blumer felt this event as a severe blow to her expectations and plans for her winter's social campaign. As had been her custom in the past, she had returned to town "during the horribly torrid weather," she explained to her intimates, "for the express purpose" of getting *her* house in readiness for the season's first affair. Now the thought that "two young things" had anticipated her "was most exasperating, *most* exasperating!"

I admired the Duanes' taste in abstaining from flourishing the particulars of their dance in the columns of the press.—Social events should not be advertised like business enterprises.—Mrs. Blumer frequently sent the society editors more material than they could find space for. This I have heard on good authority.

Well, as I have said, I was among the first guests to arrive at the Duane dance.

Outdoors, that evening, it was rainy and disagreeable. People who had carriages came in them. A conveyance was at the door when I ascended the steps, and it was Mrs. Blumer's, for I heard that lady's voice in loud conversation. Embarrassed at the thought of meeting the mother of the girl toward whom I had so abruptly ceased my attentions, I hurried into the house. Nor was I a moment too soon, for Mrs. Blumer followed closely. As I made my way through the hall and to the staircase, I overheard her remark to a companion,—

" Yes, I have come, though, really, I was undecided whether I should do so, until the last moment. I am here because I felt it my duty to society."

Dancing did not begin for some little time, and in the reception room there pervaded an awkward uncertainty of what to do and say. People stood about in groups, nodding and smiling at one another's every remark. The hostess, a charming girl, was surrounded by a lot of old ladies who were praising her every action, in even monoto-

nous voices. I moved about, and chatted
with various people.

As time passed, and as the room began to
fill with more frequent arrivals, I could not
help wondering—though I wished to avoid
her—why Mrs. Blumer did not make her
appearance. She had come so early, and
she was yet absent from the reception room!
I asked myself how I should feel when I
encountered Miss Blumer. I could not
imagine. I judged, and I think rightly, that
Mrs. Blumer waited that she might make
her entry into a well-filled room. At length
I heard her name and that of her daughter
announced together with the names of a
number of others. Mrs. Blumer appeared
upon the scene, accompanied by several
young men; these were her retainers, who
acted at various functions in the capacity
of her social servants. They fluttered hither
and thither at her bidding. When she was
unnoticed by the beaux and leaders, she
had them at her beck and call to surround
her, and to keep her "a success." Mrs.
Blumer also brought with her several of

the more conspicuous débutantes—girls who rouged and were actressy in dress and in manner. Their duty it was to talk and tell of Mrs. Blumer's entertainments. They extolled her as " *the* " social leader, and implied that her house was the place of meeting for all society. Mrs. Blumer kept those in her social employ remunerated. She carried accounts with the leading jewelers. She ran these accounts by a system of occasional small payments *on* account, and the return of numerous and costly jewels taken for inspection, but rarely actually purchased. Those débutantes fortunate enough to be in the employ of Mrs. Blumer always had the latest things in jewelry supplied them free of charge, for their personal adornment.

When the music commenced we were ushered into the private ball-room. It was spacious, and fitted throughout in costly hard woods. In its brilliant illumination it resembled an old baronial hall. Mrs. Duane started the dancing with Van Dennis: he had come over specially from New York for that evening.

I TOOK UP MY POSITION NEAR THE DOOR AND WATCHED THE PASSERS-BY.

The floor became awhirl with beautifully gowned women and their partners. And, as I am not a dancing man—which I have before remarked—I took up my position near the door and watched the passers-by. There went Ashton, a man of the butterfly style, flitting about from place to place; he was bowing in a manner of condescension to those he passed, and stopping ever and anon to speak words of encouragement to a favored few.

Here came that happy member of society, the grinner, with face continually immersed in smiles; what a pleasant thing to feel always in joyous mood!

I saw the set-phrase conversationalist who, armed with his schedule of topics and funny stories, faced the ladies and, with appropriate gesticulations and modulations, recited to them that which he had previously memorized. Again, the patronizing man, who slapped his masculine friends on their backs, talked in a stentorian voice, and "got off" poor jokes. The society martyr who made *mal-à-propos* remarks: in consequence of which he was cut by every other acquaintance.

The awkward man, who caught his feet in ladies' trains, stumbled through the dances, had a faculty of spilling things upon one during supper time, and of rendering his presence a general nuisance.

The contortionist, or young lady who endeavors to make herself attractive by rolling her eyes, and jumping up and down.

At length I tired of posing as an onlooker; so I mingled with the non-dancing procession and drifted around the room. Near the walls and interspersed among the plants and flowers were to be seen, here and there, varieties of that artificial growth flourishing at dances—the wallflowers.

On several occasions I separated myself from the promenaders, to join a friend or an acquaintance. I had a tête-à-tête with a girl who affected the grandiose mode of speech: she referred to her one day's trip to Washington as, " When we were south this summer," and spoke of her visit to New York as, " The stupid time I had over there."

I stopped before the off-eyed beauty, but, after a futile attempt at making her look at me when she talked, I passed on to Miss O'Neil, who was biting her lips and showing her dimples.

Next I chatted with Miss Florence, an enthusiastic young lady, whose art of entertaining consisted in bewildering one by her profuseness and over-appreciation.

In duty bound, I spoke to the frank girl: she told me that she bored people, and that men were only attentive to her for her mother's sake.

She was informing me of my own faults, in an obliging manner, when I found myself called elsewhere.

On passing a group of people who were pronouncing Miss Blumer the belle of the evening, I chanced to espy this lady among the dancers. As I looked she caught my eye, and smiled. "Now," I thought, "I am in for it!" Miss Blumer guided herself to her chair. I tried to escape her further attention. But her eyes were upon me. I felt them, and I was compelled to glance in her direction. Immediately she nodded. There was nothing left to me but to join her. She was seated beside Miss Thornton, a great friend of Miss Emily Tracy's.

"Ah! Good-evening, ladies," I said by way of greeting.

Miss Blumer smiled bewitchingly, while Miss Thornton answered my salutation pleasantly, but reservedly.

"How do you do, Mr. Hall? I am so delighted to see you, you deserter!" Miss Blumer said. " Do sit down here, and talk to me. That is, though, if you can spare the time. You are in such demand that I fear what I ask will be a self-sacrifice on your part."

"Why, how absurd, Miss Blumer!" I stammered.

"Not absurd at all, Mr. Hall," Miss Blumer went on. "You underestimate yourself, I assure you. Why, you are the admiration of all the girls and the envy of every man here."

I grinned uncomfortably. "Oh, you are joking."

Miss Thornton glanced disdainfully at Miss Blumer, and then turned to me:—

"Aren't you going to speak a word to me, Mr. Hall?"

"Why, of course," I returned. "But Miss Blumer has been flattering me to such an extent that I haven't had a chance to say anything, as yet."

Miss Thornton replied significantly,—

"You mustn't believe all she says: she is only in fun, you know."

Hereupon Miss Blumer glared at Miss Thornton, and I became embarrassed.

"Don't you love waltzing?" asked Miss Blumer, as the orchestra struck up.

"Yes," I answered absently.

"Oh, I do detest waltzes; don't you?" Miss Thornton said, as if unconscious of the previous remark.

"Yes indeed," I assented. Then, recalling suddenly the reply I had just given Miss Blumer, I stammered, "That is to say, I —— — —"

"Oh, I understand perfectly," Miss Thornton remarked. She looked at me

10

amusedly, coyly, and yet with interest. I
wished to speak with her about Miss Tracy,
so, as a would-be partner presented himself
to Miss Blumer, I asked,—

"Will you promenade?"

The remainder of the evening I spent in
company with Miss Thornton. Of course
she was not cognizant of my love for the
girl of whom we talked. The subject to
her was a welcome one, for she was a devoted admirer of her friend. Miss Thornton
had already received a letter from Emily.
It was dated in Paris, where she and her
aunt were making a brief stay in order
to get thoroughly rested before renewing
their journey to Baden-Baden. Emily was
not yet equal to undergoing great fatigue,
though the change of travel had already
proved highly beneficial to her. She had
not stated how long they would remain in
Germany.

"She tries to hide her troubles from her
best friends," Miss Thornton said. "The
dear girl has had a dreadful blow, even from
the shock of which I fear it will take her a
long time to recover."

We both talked with great feeling of the Tracys, recalling many pleasant memories of our intimate friends who were no more. Miss Thornton's eyes overflowed with tears when I referred to Emily's sister.

"Gertrude was indeed a noble woman," she said. "Her action in rescuing Emily was not only sisterly but glorious. She was a brilliant girl and full of promise. I loved her and admired her, but Emily has ever been my best and dearest friend."

When I parted from Miss Thornton I felt better in mind and spirit. The evening had not been without benefit to me. As I returned to my boarding house, through the gray dawn of early morning, I experienced a sense of exhilaration rather than of weariness.

CHAPTER IV.

HER LETTER, AND HOW IT INFLUENCED ME.

MY DEAR MR. HALL:

Your letter was forwarded from London, and I found it waiting my arrival at *l'Hôtel Continental*, Paris, where my aunt, Miss Stanley, and I stopped en route to Baden. To begin with, please accept my thanks for your kind expression of sympathy in my sorrow.

I have thought of all you write me, and I am greatly complimented. But as I never before so much as knew that you *cared* for me, I feel sure that you will forgive me, and appreciate my position, when I tell you that I must take a long time to consider and decide.

Aunt May and I leave shortly for England, whence we shall go far south, for the remainder of the winter. In the spring we shall return to Baden and then, if you still wish to, you may join us.

I will give you your answer when I see you. Till then I remain,

Yours very sincerely,

EMILY TRACY."

This was the long-expected letter. How I reread it, and how I pondered over its every word, I will not describe. Why, oh why, had she not given me permission to join her right away? Did she not know that I would follow her to the ends of the world? A winter of suspense, and to be away from her, was terrible to contemplate. Still, my commands had come. I must obey them.

Now I felt more strongly than ever the necessity of employing my time. I again renewed my interest in the lace-importing scheme. Calling upon Tyndall with reference to the matter, I was taken aback at his lack of enthusiasm. He did not seem so eager to begin the enterprise as he had been

at first. At this I wondered. But I was
not deterred from my own determination to
go ahead. Tyndall's changeableness both-
ered me, but I attributed it to his peculiar
disposition.

Under the circumstances, I could not bear
the thought of spending the winter in Philadelphia. I set about making immediate
arrangements for a voyage to Madeira. No
longer would I delay my visit to the graves
of my mother and father. To Messrs.
Falck & Co., New York, I wrote to secure
passage by one of the Insular Navigation
Company's vessels sailing to Madeira. But
before I posted this letter I found myself in
receipt of a communication from London.
Tearing open the envelope, I thought it to
be from Miss Stanley's bankers and telling
me of the new address. To my surprise it
was not. The envelope contained a letter
from a friend of mine, a junior partner of
another London banking firm. He told me
important news concerning a contemplated
"drop" in certain foreign securities which
had been left me by my uncle and which I

still held. In view of this information, I
decided to go direct to London and investigate business prospects there for myself, after
which I could take ship for Madeira. I took
passage on the steamship Normania, and,
after an uneventful voyage, duly reached
Plymouth. Having been landed, I journeyed thence to London without delay. I
had intended putting up at the Charing
Cross Hotel, near the railroad station at
which I should later take the train for Southampton. But my friend, the banker, insisted
upon my stopping at his house. Frank
Simpson (that was his name) had married a
distant cousin of mine. She had not been
home to America since her marriage.

I found that I was indebted to Simpson
for a valuable piece of information. With
his aid I disposed of my foreign holdings
(later I was glad that I had done so). I
engaged passage on the steamship Trojan,
booked to sail shortly from Southampton.
At Messrs. Brown Brothers' I ascertained
nothing satisfactory. They had been notified that Miss Stanley was going south, but

where they did not know. She and Miss Tracy were moving constantly from place to place.

Early in the morning of the day of sailing, I bade my kind London friends goodbye, and departed for Southampton. The vessel left her wharf at high tide, one o'clock. For two hours she steamed down Southampton Bay under the guidance of the pilot. That worthy disembarked when we entered the English Channel.

I had a stateroom companion, a Mr. Benjamin, of London. He was a Jew, as the name might serve to indicate. When I went below I stumbled over him as he was stretched full length upon the floor.

"Searching for a collar button," he remarked cheerfully; and, rising, he proceeded to introduce himself:—

"You are my companion as far as Madeira, sir: by name Mr. Hall, I believe? Yes, Mr. George Lefferts Hall, of Philadelphia, Pennsylvania, U. S. A."

"I am," I replied.

"Well, sir, hope we'll get along together. I

saw your name on the ship's passenger book. That's how I knew it. My name's Benjamin, Isaac Benjamin, of London, and I'm bound for Cape Town, Africa."

Such was my meeting with the cabin mate who was destined to open my eyes to my future.—Mr. Benjamin's only visible luggage consisted in a small hand satchel, which he had stowed carefully away. Thus I was left ample room for spreading out my own belongings.

The first morning out I was awakened at an early hour by a bumping sound directly above me. Mr. Benjamin occupied the upper berth. I clambered from mine to ascertain what might be going on. The Hebrew gentleman was seated upright; he was in the act of polishing an ancient pair of celluloid cuffs. As he scrubbed away he brought his head and elbows in contact alternately with the wall and the screw closing the porthole. Hence the cause of the noise which had aroused me from slumber. I called to Mr. Benjamin, who greeted me cheerily. He seemed in no wise disconcerted either by his cramped position or by being discovered at such occupation.

"I'm at my washing," he said, as he moistened a kerchief in his mouth and applied it (the kerchief) with renewed vigor to his wrist wear. "See," he continued, exhibiting a yellow looking collar and a false shirt front, "they are of the same material. I save at least £20 (twenty pounds) per year by having no washerwomen's bills. In fact, all my underclothing is made of a composition similar to celluloid."

I will leave it to my readers to imagine for themselves the state of my feelings on hearing this announcement.

"Where is your trunk?" I inquired. I had wanted to ask this question before. Mr. Benjamin looked gravely at me. He reminded me of an old poll-parrot on a perch, as he sat up in his bunk, his small keen eyes peering over his curved, beaky nose.

"Young man," he said, in an impressive voice, "I never had a trunk in my life. As

for travelling with one : the mere idea of
such a thing is extravagant. Why, I had
as lief travel with an invalid as with a trunk.
You're just as helpless with it. Every time
a trunk is moved its owner must dive into
his pocket for a tip. I am not the possessor
of a trunk because I could not carry it myself. That valise there is quite portable. It
contains all I have brought with me."

As I was preparing to "turn in" again
a book came crashing down on the floor
beside me.

"Hit you?" asked Mr. Benjamin, leaning
over.

"No," I replied.—I picked up the book,
and read its title,—"A Self-Made Man."
Why, it was a work of the late Mr. Stedman
Tracy's ! I said nothing directly pertaining
to it as I tossed it back to Benjamin. But
I asked him if he had ever "crossed the
herring pond." To my surprise, he said,—

"Oh, bless me, yes ; I've been to *New
York*, and I've been to Philadelphia also. I
used to be in business in New York. I liked
it better than Philadelphia, you know, as

there is so much more life there. By the
way, I remarked that you looked at that
book of mine. It is written by one of
your great Americans. That's an author's
copy too, if you please."

"What!" I cried, "you knew Mr. Tracy?"

"Knew him? I know him!"

"He's dead," I said.

At this I thought the Israelite would fall
on top of me.

"Dead!" he called, "dead? My old friend
dead? You knew him? Tell me of him."

Seeing that Mr. Benjamin was really sincere in his earnestness, and that he waited
for me to speak, I did not hesitate: I gave
him a brief account of the disastrous fire.
He listened intently. When I had concluded he made no attempt at speaking for
several moments. At length he heaved a
deep-drawn sigh, and said aloud, though
apparently to himself,—

"Ah, my dear, dear friend, I loved you! I
admired you. You liked a man for his personal worth, not for who he was. You were
independent. If I was ever near renouncing

my faith it was because *your* doctrines were so convincing, so true! You were the only Christian I ever cared for or placed absolute faith in."

A short silence again followed, and then old Benjamin leaned over his berth and held his copy of "A Self-Made Man" out toward me.

"Look on the fly leaf, Mr. Hall," he said, "look!"

I took the book and opened it at the place designated. There was an inscription in Mr. Tracy's handwriting. It read, "To my good friend Isaac Benjamin, in token of my high esteem for him, and also in appreciation of his very keen insight in discovering a scamp."

"That's odd, isn't it?" remarked Mr. Benjamin, from aloft.

"Well, rather," I replied. "Might I be so bold as to inquire its signification?"

"Certainly, and I will tell you," came the rejoinder. "You see it was this way: I went to Philadelphia knowing no one. I had an introduction to Mr. Tracy from a mutual English acquaintance, however. I duly presented this introduction, and Mr. Tracy was very kind to me. A friendship kindled between us. He seemed to like queer folks. Mr. Tracy loaned me some money to invest in my business. This was what I was sorely in need of, capital! I doubled Mr. Tracy's money. Still he left it with me. I became rich in having it at hand, ever ready to apply where it was needed. My business prospered. At last I made Mr. Tracy take back his money together with half the accumulations it had made. He had handed to me $10,000. I now returned to him $25,000. Our business transactions made us closer friends than ever.

"There was in my employ a young man in whom I had placed great confidence. I picked him up in New York, and I established him as manager of the New York branch of my business. He seemed to me a worthy fellow, and I was sorry he had few friends. I took him out to see Mr. Tracy and his charming family one time. I felt proud of him, for he was an able young man. Well, Mr. Tracy took a fancy to him; after

that he used to run over often to see Mr.
Tracy's daughters. He became a regular
visitor out at that beautiful country place.
He fell in love with Miss Emily. Now, this
would not do. The Tracys had befriended
the young man, but they wouldn't tolerate
him in the light of a suitor for their daughter's hand. Still they might have remained
too long a time in ignorance of my young
man's serious intentions, had I not, myself,
discovered the matter to my friend, Mr.
Tracy.

"I will skip over particulars; but would
you believe that this young scamp was a
hypnotist? He secretly confessed to Miss
Emily his love for her. And she would
not have him. Then he actually set about
to hypnotize her into a state of acquiescence.
As I have said, I was the first to learn of
this. The young man was discharged from
my employ, and was forbidden ever calling
again at the Tracy's. So we heard the last
of him."

"What was his name?" I gasped, scarcely
able to control my fury.

"Well, that makes little difference to you, I fancy," said Mr. Benjamin. "But still, if you *want* to know his name, it was Tyndall."

"James Brown Tyndall?" I cried.

"His full title, and pray do you know him?" said Mr. Benjamin. "If so, I don't envy you your acquaintance."

I thought I should have a fit.—Never in my life have I experienced a greater shock than I felt at that moment when the unexpected news crashed against my mind and sensibilities.—Then a flood of light seemed to rush into my memory, and to clear up all the dark places left by former doubts and perplexities. From the time of my first acquaintance with Tyndall he had been playing me false. Of course he had always taken pains to deter me from my visits to the Tracys, since he himself was a forbidden guest. It was now also plain why Tyndall had wished to turn my marriage intentions from Miss Emily to Miss Blumer. But what a low hound he had been not to face me with his complaints in the first place, like a man! . . . His continued apparent friendship for me up to the time of my departure from America I felt boded me no good.

Of course further sleep was now impossible. I dressed, and went on deck. The clear, salt air was keen and penetrating. It blew away the feverish heat generated in me by my recent excitement and cabin-stuffiness. As my temples cooled my mental condition changed. A chill passed through me, and I felt relieved in mind and body. I was my normal self again. The sun had just risen, and hung red and cold looking above the sea. The vessel plunged along, half through, half over, the surging billows, and the atmosphere forward was damp with dashing spray. Though the barefooted sailors were scrubbing decks and playing the hose freely, I contrived to find a comparatively dry and sheltered nook in which to place my steamer chair.

The remainder of the day I passed pleasantly, and without special incident. There were some British regulars bound for a military station in South Africa. It furnished amusement to the cabin passengers

11

to watch these fellows playing at games and
tricks upon the lower deck, where they were
quartered.   By the third day people were
settled down to enjoy the monotony of the
voyage.   Sufferers from *mal de mer* began
to appear on deck, swathed in shawls and
steamer rugs.   These soon found such
covering unnecessary, however, as the vessel
entered and sped through southern waters.
The air became warm and balmy, and the
sea smooth as the proverbial mill pond.

At midday we were reported to be directly off Lisbon;* though, as we skirted
the Portuguese coast at a distance of some
two hundred miles, the aspect of "water,
water everywhere" remained unaltered.

In the afternoon the starboard deck was
cleared for a game of cricket.   Spreading
nets were hoisted round about to prevent loss
overboard of the ball.   How many nation-
alities were represented among the men con-
stituting the opposing elevens, that day, I
cannot remember to a certainty.   But I know

* Lisbon, Portugal, is the nearest European port to
Madeira.

there were Spaniards, Portuguese, Germans, Swedes, English, Scotch, and French. And all were familiar, more or less, with the British national game. Mr. Benjamin proved himself an excellent batsman. It was amusing to see his son, a tall foppish fellow, endeavoring to bowl him out when his turn before the wickets arrived. In spite of considerable slipping about, muffing the ball, and personal colliding, a very jolly afternoon was spent by participants, as well as onlookers.

The following evening—the last before reaching Madeira—a ball was given in honor of those soon to leave the ship. About the upper decks, Japanese lanterns swung from lines extended between unhung awning poles,* and their light discovered numerous decorations of flag drapery. The moon, in full splendor, shone from the cloudless heavens, and dancers were sprinkled with its silvery beams.

---

* For first cabin passengers' comfort, as the vessel nears the tropics, awnings are spread above the decks exposed to the sun's direct rays.

Next morning I was wakened by a confusion of noises. The atmosphere of the ship seemed to have changed overnight. Passage-ways resounded with voices and hurrying footsteps; overhead was a heavy grating noise, as of baggage being dragged about deck. There was little vibration from machinery, and, as I listened, I realized that the engines were working very slowly. Rising, I quickly attired myself.

"We must be arriving," I said, reaching up and shaking Mr. Benjamin.

"Very good, very good," came the sleepy response. "Go out an' see the sights for me."

Such lack of enthusiasm made me impatient. I lost no time in going above. Never shall I forget the scene which greeted my eyes as I then stepped out upon the Trojan's deck. Before my sea-weary vision towered a beautiful, green, mountain isle. Across the shining water, and bathed in the mist of early morning, it appeared like some place of enchantment. A white and yellow city stretched, from a curving beach, inland

through a verdant valley, and up the sides
of gentle sloping mountains surrounding
the valley.

In other places higher mountains rose
precipitously, and tossed their snow summits
into the clouds. Against these earth and
rock monsters the rising sun shot its red
rays, causing a weird effect of lights and
shadows. Our ship had cast anchor at
about six hundred yards' distance from the
city front. We lay in Funchal Bay and
before the city of Funchal.

From the water, on all sides, arose a din
of wrangling voices. Looking over the
vessel's side, I saw the water to be alive with
small boats. Some of them were filled with
Madeiran country folk who screamed,
"Wares for sale," in broken English or
in their own lingo.

Others of the smaller boats contained
swarthy, almost naked fellows, black haired
and shiny, olive skinned. They dangled
their feet overboard, and whenever a coin
was tossed by an amusement seeking passenger into the water, they dived thither, and

contested for it below surface. For a shilling, one of the divers, more daring than the others, offered to jump from midway up the mast, clear of the ship, into the water, and thence to swim under the ship's hull. The amount which he had asked was raised. The fellow thereupon clambered with monkey-like agility onto the deck, and up into the rigging to the position whence he had promised to dive. Here he poised himself, and then he shot out head first, through the air. His body just cleared the vessel's side and, falling, cleft the water swiftly and with scarce a splash, like an arrow shot true from a bow. The ship's onlookers rushed across the deck. After a wait of about a minute and a half, the diver's head bobbed up unconcernedly. The fellow had accomplished his feat.

It was several hours before the health officers came aboard. When they did so, some large rowboats put out from shore and drew quickly alongside. Each of these crafts contained a hotel proprietor or agent. I hurried below to get my hand luggage

and to bid farewell to my cabin companion.
I found him in the saloon, seated, opposite
his son, at a small table. The two were
engaged in earnest discussion as to the
present state of the South African money
market. I asked them if they had been on
deck.

"No, we have not," they answered. "Madeira is not financially interesting to us."

I wished my friend, Mr. Benjamin, *bon voyage* to the Cape, bade him and his son
"good-bye," and, without further delay, set
about to disembark.

"Everything here, sir?" asked the proprietor of the Hotel Bella Vista, as I seated
myself in his boat.

"Everything," I replied.

"Very well, we will go then," said my
future host. He addressed his crew, two
brawny natives. Long sweeps were immediately dipped, and we pulled away from
the Trojan. As we neared the shore I saw
that waves were breaking and dashing spray
high into the air. But our boat was skillfully beached on the crest of a breaker.

Those bound for Hotel Bella Vista—two ladies and two men, including myself—were led through a crowd of gaping natives to a *carro* stand. Here we were accorded the choice of a ride to our destination in a carro (a *bullock cart*, or sort of gaudily adorned summer sledge, on runners) or in a *rede* (a hammock slung from a pole which is supported at either end by a carrier). From inexperience we all chose the carro for our transportation. Subsequently I found the rede the superior conveyance for ease and comfort, and equally as safe as the carro, for the rede bearers are a strong and sure footed set of men.

Our hotel was situated at an elevation outside and overlooking the town, and a pleasant, novel ride was afforded us thither. The streets, made of tiny cobblestones, closely packed, are kept well greased and oiled to permit of the easy sliding of runnered vehicles. Our worthy host, whose manners were the acme of politeness, designated to us places of interest along the route. In due time we reached the hotel.

I was shown to my room, where I prepared to indulge in a brief rest before breakfast. Previous to my morning repast, however, a servant entered, bearing a tray containing oranges, bananas, fresh figs, guava jelly, and tea.

PART III.

Here, in this island small, was all the treasure
    I'd gone abroad to find:
Indeed, a wondrous paradise of pleasure
    I once had left behind.

CHAPTER I.

IN THE ISLAND OF MADEIRA.

Now I will omit an account of the events which took place during my first three months' sojourn in the island. Though I accomplished much in the way of sight-seeing during this interval, the particulars of such doings would break the thread of my narrative if here chronicled. Therefore, let this statement suffice: I made frequent visits to the graves of my parents; I investigated the lace business.

The time of which I would write in detail is the occasion of my return from a visit to the island of Porto Santo.* Fresh from the sea trip in the little steamer, Lobo, I felt the

---

* This island (Porto Santo) lies about twenty-three miles northeast of Madeira. It is six and one-third miles long, and from two to three miles across.

Although settled more than four centuries ago, its population to-day numbers all told scarcely two thousand persons. Nearly all of these live in the one and only town, Villa

desire to stretch my limbs. So I set off to "foot it" to my hotel. When I had passed the outskirts of the town, and was walking along the less frequented stretch of country road leading to Hotel Bella Vista, my attention was arrested by a piercing scream. The voice was unquestionably that of a woman, and, as I listened, the sound of an approaching carro caught my ear. Whether this was whence the scream had come I could not tell. I stepped to the roadside and waited.

The carro was approaching rapidly; and I could see the oxen moving at a shambling trot, as they drew the sledge conveyance into sight, around a distant bend. I stood in a position where I might peer in at the occupants as they drove up. To my surprise, however, the curtains were all drawn. Not a sound came from within as the carro

Baleira. An administrator is stationed in Villa Baleira, who rules over this stationary population.

The only communication which these literally "insular" people have with the outside world is through a single small coasting steamer, which plies between Madeira and Porto Santo twice every month, conveying the mails and affording a means of transportation.

dashed past where I stood. The oxen-driver ran panting alongside, jabbing his tired beasts unceasingly with an iron-pointed pole. At the moment of the carro's passing I could not satisfy myself that the scream had come from it. The conveyance, after all, might be a vacant one. When I saw it disappearing behind a cloud of dust down the road, however, an overwhelming sense that everything about it was not as it should be possessed me. I ran after it, and overtook it as it was about to plunge across the bridge, towards the city.

Not knowing upon whose privacy I might be intruding, it would certainly seem rude of me to pull back the curtain. But I acted on the impulse of the moment, and of my feelings. Leaning over carefully, in order to preserve my equilibrium, I caught at the conveyance drapings. The shape of a hand from within grasped them tightly. There was then repeated a scream such as I had first heard, and this time the voice sounded familiar to me. I seized the curtains fiercely, and wrenched them back.

Was it some awful fancy that confronted me? There sat Tyndall, holding by one of his hands, in a brutal grip, the beautiful wrists of—of—Emily Tracy!

Frenzied with madness, I sprang into the moving carro and seized Tyndall by the throat. He released his hold on Emily, who fell back into the seat beside him, weak and speechless. The look of concentrated hatred that came into Tyndall's face, as he glared helplessly up at me, is beyond my power to describe. He reminded me of some hunted beast. I spoke not a syllable, but gathered all my energy and, with one violent effort, lifted Tyndall as I held him, and threw him, headlong, from the carro. Then I looked at Miss Tracy. She had fainted away. What could it all mean? Inactive I stood, in a momentary trance of surprise, wonder, and suspicion. Then I came to a realization that the carro had stopped: its driver was standing before me in an attitude of stupid inquiry.

"She crazy wife, she crazy wife," he expostulated. "Where husband gone?"

SHE HAD FAINTED AWAY. WHAT COULD IT ALL MEAN?

"Crazy wife!" I yelled at him. "What do you mean?"

The native began to tremble; I think my tone frightened him. It was no time to palaver. I turned my attention to Miss Tracy, who had begun to show signs of returning consciousness. A slight flush suffused her pale features, and she opened her eyes faintly. Her lips moved, and she whispered,—

"James, Ja——, Mr. Hall, is that you?"

"It is; it is me, Emily!" I cried passionately. "Compose yourself; you are safe. Tell me where to drive you."

For a full minute she observed me silently and in bewilderment. Then she slowly uttered the word "Carmo," and reclosed her eyes. I directed the driver to whip up his team and to convey us to the Hotel Miles Carmo without delay. He turned slowly and unwillingly, but obeyed my instructions. I looked out of the carro, on every side, to see what had become of Tyndall. But he had disappeared, and he must have done so with considerable celerity, for the driver

12

had not seen him. I saw that Miss Tracy was in no condition to sustain conversation. Otherwise I should have plied her with questions.

"Crazy wife! what did it signify?" I deliberated. "Surely it was Miss Tracy and not *Mrs. Tyndall* on whom I had forced my escort." I shuddered. "Absurd," I reassured myself. "It is Emily Tracy. There is villainy here. Tyndall will try to escape."

Meanwhile I was obliged partially to support the girl to whose timely assistance I had come. I say, "obliged *partially* to support," because I longed to take her in my arms. I cannot say whether or not I enjoyed that unlooked-for ride. When we reached the hotel, my fair charge had recovered so far as to be able to alight from the carro and to make her way up the steps and within doors. I paid and dismissed the confused carro man. Then I followed the girl I loved. She had just met a tall, fine-looking, elderly lady, who seemed concerned for her and embraced her fondly. I stood back a space until Emily became aware of my presence. On perceiving me at hand, she beckoned me to approach.

"This is my aunt," she said. "My aunt, Miss Stanley. Aunt, let me present to you my friend, Mr. Hall."

Then Emily grew pale and faint once more, and her aunt said,—

"Mr. Hall will surely excuse us for the present."

I replied,—

"Yes, certainly."

Emily turned and looked at me.

"You will return to tea?" she asked, extending her hand. I took it.

"What of that scoundrel, Tyndall?" I inquired heatedly.

Miss Stanley started, and I thought Emily would swoon on the spot. But, though her bosom heaved and her breath came quickly, she remained standing.

"Find him, and punish him. He has insulted me," she said. "Overtake him at the harbor before he sails."

Emily and her aunt turned and left me. I rushed from the hotel on my errand of vengeance. If I found Tyndall I felt that I would kill him. Running through the streets like a madman, I quickly reached the water's edge. But one large vessel was in the bay, and it was steaming slowly out to sea, having evidently just weighed anchor. My eyes becoming accustomed to the glare, I scanned the water carefully in all directions.

At length I descried a rowboat, far out, and following in the wake of the departing steamer. "It must be Tyndall pursuing to get aboard and away," I said to myself. "I pray to Heaven that he does not escape me!" I accosted a boatman and described to him the man I was after.—He *was* in that rowboat.

"A hundred dollars to you if you overtake him!" I cried breathlessly.

The boatman's eyes sparkled, and he ran his craft down the beach. We put out from shore, each taking an oar. Skimming over the long swells, it seemed we must be gaining upon the fugitive. Never a word did I exchange with my companion oarsman, but

I felt that he was working his hardest. I rowed with the fury of a demon. The veins in my arms stood out at every stroke as if to burst. Anon I glanced over my shoulder to guide our course.—Oh, how distant we were! A mile, at least! I redoubled my efforts at my oar. The boatman kept in stroke with me. Plash-plash, plash-plash. The sound gave me comfort. It was an uneven race. The steamer was moving ever more rapidly, but the boat we were pursuing was nearly alongside. It must have wings! How could it speed thus apace? The steamer would not slacken her speed. In this I was exultant. I pulled "for dear life"—but the steamer's gangway ladder was being lowered. Then, though distance made it invisible, a rope must have been thrown the boat, for it drew up to the ladder. I saw that further rowing was useless, so I tied my coat, with nervous fingers, to the end of the oar, and jumped to my feet. Just then, ahead, I perceived a man spring from the rowboat, and land safely upon the ship's ladder. I waved my coat frantically in the air and bellowed across the water. Meanwhile the figure clambered up the ladder and disappeared. It was Tyndall, and he was escaping me. I screamed so loudly that, of a sudden, my voice broke, and I could not raise it above a hoarse whisper. Meanwhile my companion did his best, in ways similar to my own, to attract the attention of those aboard. We must have been observed; but in any event no heed was paid us. The vessel had now attained great speed, and soon she rounded a promontory of the island and was lost to view. I sank back, grinding my teeth.

"Row for the shore," I ordered, and accordingly we did so. I waited on the beach for the return of the other boat. It had a crew of three brawny fellows, and them I questioned. In return I got a full description of the passenger. It tallied in every detail with Tyndall; and there could now be no room left in my mind for doubt. I might still pursue, perhaps.

"What was the ship, and where might it be sailing?"

" The steamship Wordsworth, was bound for South America, and the route lay thither direct, the first stopping place after leaving Madeira being Rio de Janeiro."

In desperation I returned to my hotel, there to await evening, when I should again see Emily. *She* had told me to avenge her insult, and I had not succeeded in doing so. When I called at the Hotel Miles Carmo I felt crestfallen. I presented my card at the hotel office, and it was conveyed to Miss Tracy's apartment. She soon appeared, looking very pale, but withal very beautiful. In a dainty white dress, the perfection of simplicity and graceful modesty, she was indeed a vision of loveliness. As she greeted me and led me out on the veranda and into the garden, I noticed that she was agitated. I had so much to ask her that I was impatient to begin questioning. We met a number of people in the garden, but finally reached a spot where a tall growth of sugar-cane screened us from observation. Sinking down upon a bench, Miss Tracy looked at me hesitatingly, and asked,—

" Did you find him ? "

" No," I replied, reddening. " He escaped me."

" Oh, I am so glad!" Miss Tracy ejaculated, sighing. And her face brightened as though the news were a great relief to her.

This mystified me.

"Are you glad that I failed to catch the late offender?" I inquired.

" Indeed I am," was the unexpected reply, spoken with great fervor.

I felt myself choking with wrathful surprise. Miss Tracy, observing how her attitude affected me, continued,—

" Pray understand me. I have been frightened ever since you left me this morning. You looked so terrible when I told you to avenge my insult that I felt sure you would kill that villain if you encountered him. The thought of this took possession of me. I upbraided myself for having had such ungentle feelings, and for having incensed you so. And now here you are." (She smiled sweetly.) "You rescued me, and, though you did so not a moment too

soon, as it is, I am without harm of any
sort. You do not know what a weight was
lifted from my mind and conscience when
you told me that which I scarcely dared hope
to hear."

"Then you *are* glad to see me?" I said.

Miss Tracy's eyelids drooped, and her face
became suffused with a deep blush. With
a glance still downward, she said,—

"Yes, I am happy that you are here."

What further could I wish? I took my
place on the bench beside her.

"Now tell me," I said, "about your encounter with that blackguard."

My fair hostess lifted her eyes to mine.

"I will," she answered. "But first let
me inform you that I knew this man a long
time ago. I always disliked him."

I told Miss Tracy that I was well aware
of the fact; and I recounted my meeting
with Benjamin.

"Oh," she exclaimed, "how interesting!
Dear old Mr. Benjamin was a very good
friend of my father's. Poor, precious
father!" Tears gathered and coursed

down her cheeks, but, with an effort, she controlled herself. " I had accompanied a friend to her hotel, the Bella Vista, and was returning homeward when I met a carro coming from the town. I was all alone. The vehicle stopped short when it came up to me, and out jumped that dreadful creature. He began declaring love, and asked me to come with him. He told me he had bought our home at auction for me. When I showed my indifference and turned to walk away, he caught me rudely by the arm, and said, ' Aha, Missy! now I have you, and you cannot get away.' I struggled with him, and called for help. But he clapped his detestable hand over my mouth and pushed me into the carro. He held me there while he made explanation to the driver. 'This is my wife whom I came out to meet. You see plainly she is crazy. Now drive like . . . . .' He spoke very wickedly, and ordered the driver to go direct to the beach. He sprang in beside me, still roughly holding me, and, with a fiendish laugh, said, ' Soon we will be man and wife, whether you wish it or not. We are now on our way to a ship which will take us direct to South America. Henceforward you and your money are mine. I shall explain to everybody, as I did to that fellow there, that you are temporarily insane; so you might as well behave yourself.'

"I felt I should faint, when I realized that some one was running after us. There was a tugging at the drawn curtains. I screamed, and then I knew no more until you were beside me. How can I thank you?"

Miss Tracy looked at me with an expression of tenderness in her beautiful eyes. I fell on my knees before her.

"Ah, Emily, Emily," I cried tremblingly. "Must I indeed be thanked like a friend? I love you, I love you so!"

Then a joy I had never dared picture even in my imagination was mine. I held her whom I loved above all the world in my arms, as she whispered softly,—

"George, I love you."

CHAPTER II.

ADVENTURES HAPPILY TERMINATED.

Now I was a constant visitor at the hotel of my betrothed. Miss Stanley suggested that I might as well remove to the Miles Carmo—where I would be available at a moment's notice. At the time I greeted the idea as a joke, and Miss Stanley and I laughed at the embarrassment of Emily. Later, however, I re-thought of the suggestion seriously, and I decided that it was a very excellent one. So, accordingly, I packed my trunk and changed the place of my abode. At the Miles Carmo I was allotted a room in an old, distant wing. Large, airy, and on the ground floor, its two windows looked out near a side piazza, and over the garden, some ten feet below.

The evening of my coming I spent, until a late hour, in company with Emily. When,

at length, I bade her good-night and deliv-
ered her to the keeping of her aunt, I betook
myself to my bedchamber. But I did not
feel sleepy, so I lit a lamp and settled myself
to read. The windows were open, and wind
blew out the lamp flame. I lowered the
sashes, struck a match, and again kindled
the wick. Scarcely had I replaced the globe
when a breeze seemed to rise in the atmosphere directly behind me. It blew over my
shoulders. The lamp flickered and went out
as before. I looked hastily backward. The
door was closed. I had pushed the bolt after
entering. The occurrence seemed unaccountable. Once more I relit the lamp, and
opened my book.

I had read for about twenty minutes this
time before the flame was again extin-
guished. "It must be something wrong
with the burner, or a draught blowing
through a crevice in the wall," I surmised.
Feeling as yet wide awake and in no humor
for retiring, I reopened a window—the one
nearest to the piazza—and sat down to enjoy
the cool air. The book I had been reading

was "A Study in Scarlet." Having closed
the chapter of the strange murder, my mind
teemed with fancies. Dr. Doyle is assuredly
a master in the art of mystery weaving.
The hour must have been close to midnight:
not a creature seemed stirring, either within
or without doors. The side of the hotel
towered, a great, black wall—for there were
no illuminations to set off or show the windows, owing to the lateness.

A rustle below, in the foliage, attracted my
attention. I peered down, and was greatly
surprised to see a typical old-fashioned gentleman in a high, white beaver hat, brass-
buttoned coat, and stock, and indeed entire
dress of many years ago. He walked forth
from a garden path, and leisurely ascended
the hotel steps on to the veranda. There he
stood, clearly visible in the moonlight. He
was a tall, well-proportioned man, fine looking, and of dignified bearing. While study-
ing him, a rapidly moving shadow crossed
my vision. I espied a villainous-appearing
fellow stealing cautiously out of the darkness. He slunk close up to the gentleman

in the beaver, who, however, turned on hearing him.

"You are quiet, sir," the gentleman remarked sarcastically.

The newcomer replied in English, with a slight Portuguese accent,—

"Ah, good sir, perhaps. Pray could you tell me ze time ohf evening?"

The gentleman unbuttoned his coat, drew forth a watch, and was looking down to consult it when his interlocutor sprang upon him, a long knife in his hand. I leaped from my window onto the piazza. Even as I was in mid-air the assassin passed the blade across and through his victim's throat, cutting it open from ear to ear. In the same instant he plunged his other hand into the unfortunate gentleman's pocket and brought out a bundle of papers. Landing upon my feet, I clutched for the murderer. He evaded me, and faded away into air. I shivered. Was he some dread phantom? He had vanished. I knelt where I saw the body of the murdered man, and felt it. How hard it was: it seemed like wood! Rubbing my hands up and down over where it lay, they began to pain and smart; I found them filled with splinters.

Events to this juncture took place before my mind and senses as I have related. Therefore, my present situation was incomprehensible; for, glancing up and about me, I found myself on the floor of my own room. I rushed to the window. Several people were out upon the piazza. They seemed in no wise disturbed, for they were talking and laughing gayly. From their conversation I learned that they had just returned from a moonlight excursion in the country. The thought that I had awakened from a dream suggested itself. I could not remember having either closed or opened my eyes. Still, the circumstances and surroundings of the present were such as to make me discredit that which I had believed to have happened. There were no visible signs without doors of any one's having been assaulted. I retired to bed with a feeling of misgiving as to my mind —wondering whether I had wandered in it, or whether I had dreamed with my eyes open.

Next morning I inquired at the office if anything had gone wrong in the garden overnight. Receiving an answer in the negative, I asked various questions concerning my room, its location, and the history of its various former occupants. The clerk, an Englishman, eyed me quizzically. But during the course of the interview with him the hotel proprietor drew near and listened.

"By Jove!" he ejaculated, of a sudden. "Your name is Mr. Hall, isn't it? and you are an American?"

"Yes," I replied.

"Well, what you are asking so particularly about your room for I do not know; but I will tell you of a very curious coincidence," the proprietor continued. "A guest was murdered in that very room about twenty-six years ago; his last name was Hall, and he was an American—what is more, a Philadelphian. I did not own this house then, but I am told that Mr. Hall was found on the floor of his room the following day, with his throat cut. The murderer escaped, and was never captured."

"That murdered gentleman was my father," I remarked. And I turned on my heel, and left the proprietor and his clerk standing gaping in speechless amazement.

Emily and I were not together so much as usual that day. She had a fit of despondency—to which she was still subject, and during which she desired to shun the society of those for whom she most cared. It was heartrending to see the intensity of the poor girl's grief when thoughts of her father, mother, and sister recurred to her. She strove bravely to hide signs of her sorrow from others; and it was sweet to me to hear her say, "George dear, in you I find all I have lost. 'God hath taken away, but, again, God hath given.'"

I spent the morning in the garden, a place luxuriant in growths of tropical and semi-tropical fruits and flowers. In the afternoon I went down to the bankers and drew some money. Indeed I drew quite a good deal—some three hundred pounds. Returning through the Public Gardens, I felt a sensation as if I were watched or followed.

I turned sharply about, and was just in time to see a man disappearing hastily down a side path. I ran back, and caught another glimpse of him from a distance.—On first sight I had felt that I recognized him. Now I was sure of it. He looked, for all the world, like John Dooner.—It was Dooner! But why or how he had come out to Madeira it was beyond my power even to guess.

When I passed the hotel office that evening on my way to retire, an attendant was in waiting for me. The proprietor had changed my room on his own responsibility, and I was shown to my new quarters. Though still on the ground floor, and overlooking the garden, as I preferred, they were in a newer portion of the building. I raised both windows before getting into bed. Scarcely had my head touched the pillow when I fell asleep.

The next thing I knew was when I opened my eyes and found a masked man bending over me. I started up, but a towel was clapped heavily upon my face. It was saturated with chloroform. What was more, my adversary straddled me, and fought with might and main to retain the cloth where he had put it. In my violent exertions I could not but draw deep breaths, and so my lungs were quickly filled with the narcotic exhalations. In less time than it takes to tell I was unconscious. I revived in the glare of broad daylight and arose, giddy and nauseated. My trunk had been opened, as had my strong box. The locks were forced, and my money, three hundred pounds, was gone.—An idea struck me: I thought of the time I had discovered John Dooner spying upon Emily and me. Thoughts of this had also recurred to my mind when Mr. Benjamin told his story. Then I suspected, and now I felt certain that Dooner was Tyndall's accomplice. As Tyndall had once set him to watch and report concerning my attentions to Emily, so he had now evidently set him to commit burglary upon me.

I lost no time in notifying the hotel proprietor of my loss; and, furthermore, I visited the American consul, and made complaint to the police authorities through him. I had

not recognized the thief, but I furnished
Dooner's description to the police. Yet,
though a watch was stationed at the harbor
to prevent Dooner's escape from Madeira,
and though I had the assurance of the authorities that no efforts should be spared to
find and catch the burglar, he was not se-
cured. He eluded all pursuit. And how he
succeeded remains to be told.

Emily and I made a number of excursions
together to points of interest along the coast
and in the interior. It had been at first proposed to go to Baden Baden in the spring,
but now we all found ourselves impatient to
return to America. So, when the time came
for leaving, we took ship for Liverpool,
and thence again to New York, which we
reached after a delightful voyage.

Miss Stanley took Emily direct to Chicago
with her. I went to Philadelphia.

REMINISCENCE.

HAVING completed arrangements for our marriage, which was to be solemnized at Miss Stanley's house, I found it impossible to absent myself longer from my betrothed. Needless to say, the several weeks of our separation, following the return from abroad, had passed too slowly for me. Though Miss Stanley favored a long engagement, I finally prevailed upon her to sanction our being joined in the fall. So on the noon of October 3, 188-, Emily and I were made man and wife. Only a few intimate relatives and friends were invited to the wedding, it being necessarily a "quiet affair." Nevertheless, Miss Stanley's mansion was the scene of a very happy little party. Miss Thornton was Emily's maid of honor, and Duane acted as my best man. His young wife, always sweet and merry, was the fun- and mischief-maker of the occasion. Our car-

riage presented a far from staid appearance
when my bride and I rolled off that afternoon. We suspected Mrs. Duane's having
been one of its chief decorators.

Emily and I had planned to spend our
honeymoon on a trip to California. We
journeyed direct to San Francisco, where we
stopped for a week or so at the Baldwin
Hotel. Then, tiring of city sight-seeing, we
took a jaunt down to San Rafael. As our
steamer moved across the bay we could see,
far off, through the entrance of the Golden
Gate, the whitecaps of the broad Pacific.
We passed near the fortifications of the Al-
cartraz, towering forbiddingly in mid-harbor.
Landing at Sansalito, we took the train; and
the entertainment afforded us from the car
window in watching the grand and ever-
changing scenery made the short ride all *too*
short. An hour after leaving the wharf at
the foot of Market Street, San Francisco,
found us installed at Hotel Rafael, San
Rafael. We whiled away the afternoon in
an excursion by the Scenic Railway to the
summit of Mount Tamalpais. This adjacent

eminence commands a view from the sky-bordered ocean to the cloud-bathed Sierras.

That evening, after our return, as my wife and I were seated at dinner, a noticeable couple came into the dining room and took a table near us. I did not see them for some time, as my back was turned, so I shall quote from Emily's description as she gave it, facing them and me :—

A petite but dashing-looking girl, of the Spanish type, with flashing eyes, wavy, black hair, and of olive complexion, was accompanied by a short, ugly man, her evident lover. My wife remarked that he regarded the girl with an earnestness denoting rapture and devotion. From their manner, Emily judged them to be townspeople. They ordered some light refreshment. Having finished, they pushed out their chairs and arose to depart. My curiosity here got the better of me, and I turned and looked : the man was Dooner!

It was not long afterwards that I went to the police station to swear out a warrant for his arrest. Several citizens were lounging

about within, as I entered. The chief of
police plied me with many questions, and
when I had given him Dooner's description,
and had furthermore supplied a brief account
of Dooner's past villainies, I could not help
noting the effect my words produced upon
one of the bystanders. He was attired in
the costume of a vaquero, and looked a full-
blooded Mexican. The fellow listened to me
eagerly, and when I had told of Dooner's
brutal and cowardly behavior towards the
woman I knew him to have wronged, the
Mexican hastily, and without a word, left
the building.

It was several hours afterwards that a
dirty envelope, addressed, in an uneven hand,
to me, was brought to our room. The bell
boy waited for an answer, stating that the
bearer of the note wished to see me, downstairs. I drew from the envelope a bit of
paper on which was written, in pencil scrawls:
"Come with José quickly. I am dying.
John Dooner."

Emily did not wish me to answer this
summons.

"It may be some dreadful plot to entrap you," she said.

But at length I obtained her rather reluctant consent, and went below. Awaiting me at the hotel doorway was the identical fellow for whom my relation of Dooner's doings seemed to have had such an extraordinary interest, in the police station. Now he showed himself to be very nervous and excited, and he greeted me with,—

"Good-night, señor. It is by you he die. You are ze cause, but w'at you say is true. My hand struck ze deathblow. Come quick."

At a loss to understand, I nevertheless hastened down the street, at the speaker's side.

"Make yourself plain," I said. "Do you mean to say that Dooner is dying at your hands?"

"My name José Valera," was the quick response. "My sister—she love, and to marry zis, w'at you call, Dooner. But I hear you tell w'at a devil he is, so I go home an' tell my sister. She not care w'at I say.

My sister tells me leave casa w'en her love, he come home. I no leave. An' we proud people, so I shoot zis Dooner. He fall, but he can speak. He say, 'Oo told you I am wicked?' I tell him, an' he sent for you."

We came before a neat little house and went in. In the hallway, and bolstered up on a chair, sat the victim of the shooting; on the floor, by his side, knelt the young girl I had seen in the Hotel Rafael dining room. She arose when we had entered, and a spirited harangue took place between José and her. She began by speaking in Spanish, but, evidently desiring what she said to be plain to all, soon branched off into English, which she spoke fluently. Turning upon me with an expression of pent-up fury, she said,—

" You, señor, are the cause of all my misfortune. I could kill you, but that I know such action would do me no good. He who was to have been my husband lies there, dying. He has told me of his folly, but I forgive him. Though he may have been false to another woman, his death will break my heart. I forgave him, and he is mine.

"I am the judge of whom I should marry. No one else is, or shall be. I want now a priest. José has summoned one. He will soon be here, and will wed us. José and I have lived happy since children. We loved each other dearly. Our parents are dead, long years. And now I hate José; I have told him so. José will give himself to the law, and if my husband dies José will hang."

Dooner interrupted,—

"Mr. Hall, I did not think I would see you again. I barely escaped them foreign devils you put after me, out in Funchal. But I did give 'em the slip, though only to be tracked by you, after all. I haven't time to ask you no questions, for my life's goin' from me fast. So I'll just talk. It was that blackleg friend of yours that made me go wrong. He had me watching your courting on that Tracy lady. He wanted you to marry the Blumer lady, as he had his 'sails set' for Miss Tracy himself. He thought he had her safely before you waylaid him in Funchal. He had hid low and planned things to get away with the lady when you were at Porto Santo. You got back too soon for his plans, though, and he left Madeira, and me to do his 'dirty work.' It was impossible for me to get Miss Tracy after Tyndall went away: you were always with her.—But if you hadn't moved to her hotel when you did, I could have kidnapped her for sure.—So I watched you draw your money at the bank one day, and robbed you of it that night. Of course I didn't send stolen goods to Tyndall, although that was the idea. When he had me with him he had a way of controlling my doings. But once away he lost his power . . ."

Here the wounded man was taken with a fit of coughing which caused a stream of blood to pour from his mouth. At this time a doctor arrived. He took the victim in hand and made an examination of his injuries. The girl stood by him the while, never flinching. José and I scurried hither and thither to give every assistance possible. The doctor worked for some two hours over his patient. Then he took José, whom he seemed to know, aside. I overheard him say,

"It is no use. The man is bleeding to death, internally. Arteries near the heart have been torn away, and operating would be of no avail. Who shot him?"

"I did," was the reply, firmly given.

The doctor looked askance.

"If he dies, as he may at any moment, you are a murderer, if you shot him intentionally."

José turned away.

"I deliver myself to ze police," he said, in a choking voice.

A drumming of hoofs was heard upon the street. The noise grew louder, and then sound indicated that several horses had been stopped in the roadway outside the cottage.

"It is ze mounted police after Dooner," José remarked. "Zey will have me instead." He cast an appealing glance of inquiry towards his sister, but she paid him no heed. With a heavy sigh, as of resigned despair, José went to the door. He flung it open in the faces of three officers. They entered.

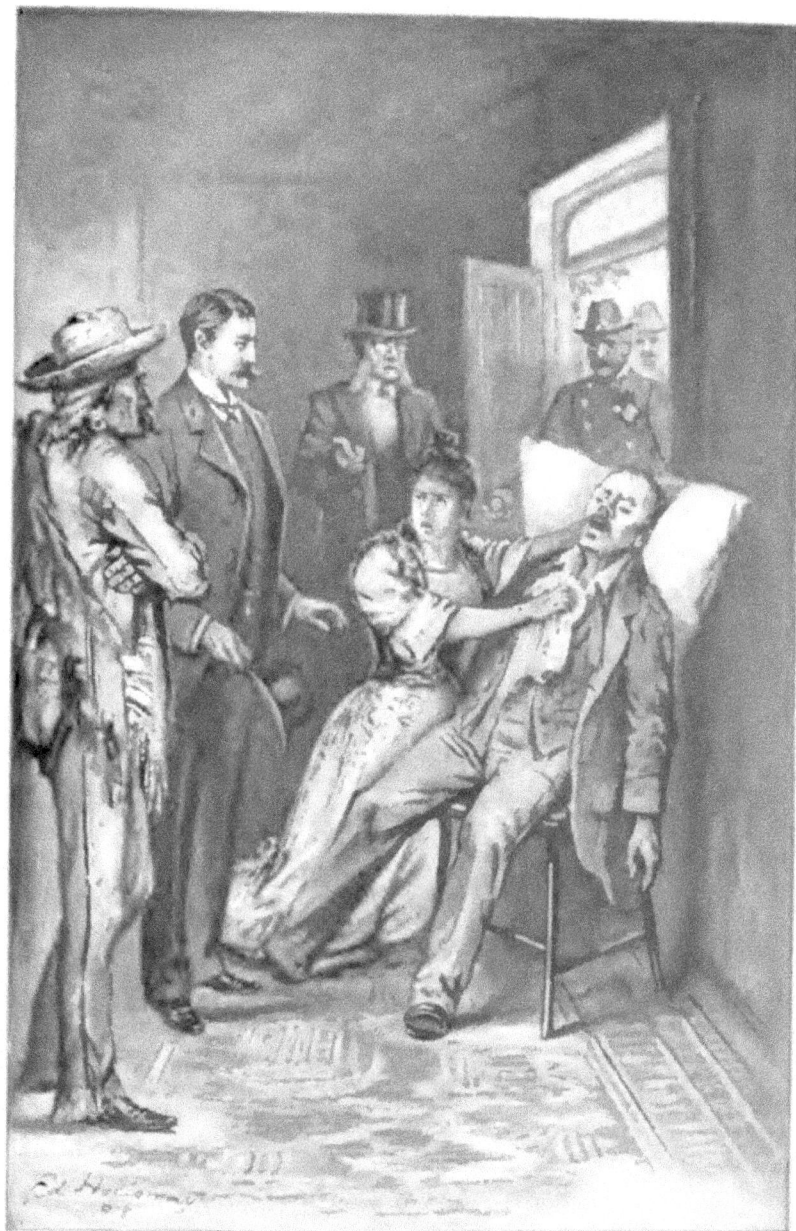

THE END OF JOHN DOONER.

"Is a feller called Dooner here?" their spokesman asked.

José answered,—

"Yes, but I shot him. Zere he is, an' he can't get away. So you needn't take him wiz you just now. Take me in hees place."

The police looked surprised. Their leader interviewed the doctor, and, receiving his report of the case, decided to leave Dooner undisturbed: he was plainly in no condition to be moved. One man was left on guard without, and the other two departed, taking José with them. No expression of sympathy came from José's sister as he was led away. Seeing my opportunity, I took my own departure, and hurried back to the hotel. Emily was anxiously awaiting me.

*   *   *   *   *

It is about a year since Emily and I returned from our wedding trip. We have settled down to housekeeping in Chicago, as Emily has quite an extensive connection here. But Philadelphia is hard to desert. Although neither of us has a relative there,

we have many, many, dear friends. Indeed
we have made several trips to Philadelphia
during the present winter.

We were reminiscent this morning, and
my wife reminded me of a matter that had
escaped my attention :—

"I was glancing through your diary recently, and, do you know, you have left off
very abruptly and unsatisfactorily," she said.

"To tell the truth, I had forgotten of the
diary's existence," I replied.

And I now resume the pen to round up
my story with the events which subsequently
happened.—

John Dooner died a short while after I
saw him, on the night of the shooting. I
read afterwards in a paper that a priest had
arrived and had performed the marriage service between him and Señorita Valera just
before his death. It was stated that the
young Mexican woman had been left some
$800 by her lover. I have not the slightest
doubt that this legacy constituted what remained of the money stolen from me. However, I made no effort at recovery, and held

my peace. I could better afford to lose the money than could Dooner's widow.

José Valera was to be tried for murder. He had been imprisoned pending his trial. But whether his sister's feelings at this time underwent a change towards him, and caused her to come to his rescue, I do not know. Perhaps, in jail, José reconsidered his action of sacrifice to his sister's wishes, and decided that freedom was more desirable. At any rate, it is some eight months since the Chicago papers contained reports of José Valera's escape from prison. I have not yet heard of his recapture. A friend, recently returned from San Rafael, informs me that rumor says his sister entered a convent.

What has become of Tyndall I do not know: I think he will never trouble me again.

IMPRIMATUR.

At the request of my wife's relatives and our intimate friends, I have had this MS. printed in book form for private distribution.

Nota Bene:

CHICAGO, ILL., April 1, 1898.

It has been a number of years since I made the foregoing note. And although much has since happened—for whose life, at any period, is *without* incident?—still, that early part of my life of which I have written perhaps makes a narrative sufficiently complete in itself to interest the disinterested. At least, so a publishing friend of mine has thought. For, since I presented a copy of my privately printed book to him, he has constantly been bothering me for permission

to issue an edition for public circulation.
Now that this edition appears, I can only
hope that the public may not condemn me
for having yielded to the temptation to see
myself in print.

GEORGE LEFFERTS HALL.

www.ingramcontent.com/pod-product-compliance
Lightning Source LLC
Chambersburg PA
CBHW030328270326
41926CB00010B/1542